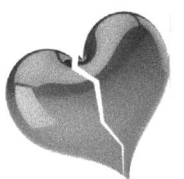

BEING HAPPY TOGETHER
What to Do to Keep Love Alive

The Secrets of Happy Relationships Series

DR. LAURIE WEISS

Empowerment Systems Books

Being Happy Together
What to Do to Keep Love Alive
The Secrets of Happy Relationships Series
Dr. Laurie Weiss
© 2019 Laurie Weiss

All rights reserved. No part of this book may be reproduced in any form or by any electronic or mechanical means, including information storage and retrieval systems, without permission in writing from the publisher, except by a reviewer who may quote brief passages in a review.

The author has done her best to present accurate and up-to-date information in this book, but she cannot guarantee that the information is correct or will suit your particular situation.

This book is sold with the understanding that the publisher and the author are not engaged in rendering any legal, medical, or any other professional services. If expert assistance is required, the services of a competent professional should be sought.

First published as Being Happy Together: How to Create a Fabulous Relationship with Your Life Partner in Less Than an Hour a Week

Library of Congress Control Number: 2018914696
Paperback 978-1-949400-18-2
Ebook 978-1-949400-19-9
Downloadable audio file 978-1-949400-20-5

Books may be purchased in quantity by contacting the publisher directly at:

Empowerment Systems Books
506 West Davies Way
Littleton, CO 80120 USA
Phone 303.794.5379
LaurieWeiss@EmpowermentSystems.com
www.EmpowermentSystems.com

Cover: Nick Zelinger, www.NZGraphics.com
Interior Design: Istvan Szabo, Ifj.
Family & Relationships / Marriage & Long-Term Relationships / Self-Help

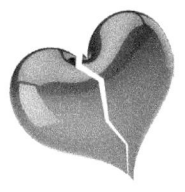

Special Bonus

Listen to a wide-ranging conversation about relationships as radio host Steve Toth interviews Dr. Laurie Weiss on his *Mind, Body and Spirit* radio show.

Discover:

- Mistaken beliefs that destroy relationships
- How caring confrontation creates better communication

- Hidden agendas that lead to arguments
- Why really listening is important
- How clarifying values helps end arguments

Download your 47-minute MP3 file here and listen today.

www.BooksByLaurie.com/SteveToth

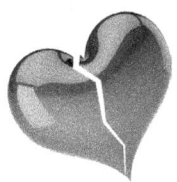

Contents

Special Bonus	3
Introduction	11
Part 1: The Challenge: Keep Your Relationship Vibrant and Growing	13
Part 2: About Relationships	31
Chapter 1: *It's OK to Be Different*	32
Chapter 2: *Your Partner Is Your Mirror*	33
Chapter 3: *Go Away, Closer*	34
Chapter 4: *Childhood Experiences Make a Difference*	35
Chapter 5: *You're Both Right*	36
Chapter 6: *Give In—Sometimes*	37
Chapter 7: *Notice What Works*	38
Chapter 8: *Recovering from Temporary Insanity*	39
Chapter 9: *Your Relationship Is Worth the Challenge*	40
Part 3: Communication	41
Chapter 10: *Courtesy Counts*	42
Chapter 11: *Give Up Mind Reading*	43
Chapter 12: *Instead of Pretending*	44
Chapter 13: *Clarity Is Powerful*	45

Chapter 14: *Don't Say Yes, Say Maybe* 46

Chapter 15: *Remember to Say "Thanks"* 47

Chapter 16: *Keep Your Agreements* 48

Chapter 17: *It's OK to Renegotiate* 49

Chapter 18: *Describe Your Own Emotions* 50

Chapter 19: *Get Permission First* 51

Chapter 20: *Listen, Listen, Listen* 52

Chapter 21: *Slow Down to Match Your Partner* 53

Chapter 22: *Ask Before You Try to Help* 54

Chapter 23: *Find Out What's Really Needed* 55

Part 4: Difficult Communication 57

Chapter 24: *Don't Delay; Talk About It—Now* 58

Chapter 25: Anger Means You Want Something to Be Different .. 59

Chapter 26: *Give Advance Warning of Unilateral Changes* 61

Chapter 27: *Break a Vicious Cycle* 62

Chapter 28: *Prove That You're Listening* 63

Chapter 29: Speak After You Listen 64

Chapter 30: *Face-to-Face May Be Too Close* 66

Chapter 31: *Careful Confrontation Works — Here's How* 67

Chapter 32: *Request Behavior Changes* 68

Chapter 33: *Let Your Partner Be Right* 70

Chapter 34: *Deliberately Create Consequences* 71

Chapter 35: *Respond Instead of Counterattacking* 72

Part 5: Play 73

Chapter 36: *Being Silly Is Good for You* 74

Chapter 37: *Touching Is Connecting* 75

Chapter 38: *Laugh With Each Other* 76

Chapter 39: *Expand Your Play Horizons* 77
Chapter 40: Go Out to Play Together 78
Chapter 41: *A Mini-vacation? Just Do It* 79
Chapter 42: *Take the Initiative Yourself* 80
Chapter 43: *What a Strange Way to Solve a Problem* 81

Part 6: Tasks **83**

Chapter 44: *Negotiate and Renegotiate* 84
Chapter 45: *Do It, Delegate It or Dump It* 85
Chapter 46: *Finish Something and Celebrate* 86
Chapter 47: *Practice Project Management* 87
Chapter 48: *Keep a List* 88
Chapter 49: *Avoid Unpleasant Surprises* 89
Chapter 50: *Do It Together* 90
Chapter 51: *Surprise Your Partner* 91

Part 7: Boundaries **93**

Chapter 52: *Do You Really Need Control?* 94
Chapter 53: *Substitute Cooperation for Control* 95
Chapter 54: *You Don't Have to Share Everything* 96
Chapter 55: *Respect Each Other's Privacy* 97
Chapter 56: *Being too Polite Causes Problems* 98
Chapter 57: *Explore the Reasons for Your Preferences* 99
Chapter 58: Make Clear Agreements—and Change Them
When Necessary 100
Chapter 59: *Insulate Your Partner from Outside Negativity* 101
Chapter 60: *Make Important Decisions Together* 102
Chapter 61: *Don't Retaliate—Period* 103
Chapter 62: *Obedience School???* 104

Part 8: Money 105
    Chapter 63: *Start by Paying Attention* 106
    Chapter 64: *Write Down the Numbers* 107
    Chapter 65: *Use a System to Track Your Information* 108
    Chapter 66: *Decide What Sharing Equitably Means* 109
    Chapter 67: *Negotiate and Renegotiate* 110
    Chapter 68: *Multiple Accounts Often Make Sense* 111
    Chapter 69: *Focus on Priorities* 112
    Chapter 70: *Work with a Financial Advisor* 114
    Chapter 71: *Getting Clear Is Better Than Getting Even* 115
    Chapter 72: *Back to Basics — Spend Less, Save More* 116
    Chapter 73: *Share Responsibility* 117
    Chapter 74: *Create Your Own Team* 118

Part 9: Special Occasions 119
    Chapter 75: *Do It, even if It Seems Unimportant* 120
    Chapter 76: *Ask for What YOU Want* 121
    Chapter 77: *Find a New Way* 123
    Chapter 78: *Meet the Family Visit Challenge* 124
    Chapter 79: *Plan Ahead to Help Each Other* 125
    Chapter 80: *Celebrate Anything You Like* 126
    Chapter 81: *Give a Hint, Take a Hint* 127
    Chapter 82: *Use Your Hints, Be a Hero* 128
    Chapter 83: Appreciate the Thought and Tell the
        Truth —Graciously 129

Part 10: Separateness 131
    Chapter 84: *Two Don't Become One* 132
    Chapter 85: *Be the Person You Are* 133

Chapter 86: *It's OK to Do Some Things by Yourself* 134
Chapter 87: *Help Each Other Grow and Change* 135
Chapter 88: *Listen When You Want to Argue* 136

Part 11: Togetherness **137**

Chapter 89: *It's Worth the Work* 138
Chapter 90: *Don't Wait, Live Now* 139
Chapter 91: *Learn Something New Together* 140
Chapter 92: *Ten Minutes Makes a Difference* 141
Chapter 93: *Imagine Being Your Partner* 142
Chapter 94: Know Your Own Priorities and Your Partner's, too 143
Chapter 95: *Practice Acts of Random Kindness* 145
Chapter 96: *When Changes Rock the Boat—Rebalance* 146
Chapter 97: *Banish Blame* 147
Chapter 98: *Nurture Each Other* 148
Chapter 99: *Heal Resentments* 149
Chapter 100: *Contribute Together* 151

Part 12: Care of Your Partner **153**

Chapter 101: *Affirm Positive Qualities* 154
Chapter 102: *Affirm Appreciated Actions* 155
Chapter 103: *Deliver a Thoughtful Surprise* 156
Chapter 104: *Focus on What's Right* 157
Chapter 105: *Promise Only What You Will Deliver* 158
Chapter 106: *Speak Your Positive Thoughts* 159
Chapter 107: *Connect with Hugs* 160
Chapter 108: *Speak in Your Partner's Love Language* 161
Chapter 109: *Discuss Important Concerns* 162
Chapter 110: *Just Listen and Be There* 163

Chapter 111: *Be Truthful About Time* 164
Chapter 112: *Compliment Publicly, Complain Privately* 165
Chapter 113: *Get Consultation When You Need It* 166
Chapter 114: *Apologize, even if It Was an Accident* 167
Chapter 115: *Listen Intensely* 168
Chapter 116: *Accept Your Partner's Feelings* 169
Chapter 117: *Empower Aliveness* 170
Chapter 118: *Avoid Known Sore Spots* 171

Part 13: Self-Care 173
Chapter 119: *Remember Your Favorite Things* 174
Chapter 120: *Include Your Personal Goals* 175
Chapter 121: *Ask for Recognition* 176
Chapter 122: *Let a Professional Help* 177
Chapter 123: *Think Before You Say Yes (or No)* 178
Chapter 124: *Pay Attention to Your Intuition* 179
Chapter 125: *Remember to Make Yourself a Priority* 180

Part 14: Your Relationship Is Worth It! 181
Special Bonus Reminder 183
Please Help Me Reach New Readers 185
About the Author 188
How to Work With Dr. Laurie 191
About the Secrets of Happy Relationships Series 195
Books in the Secrets of Happy Relationships Series 197
Other Books by Laurie Weiss 199

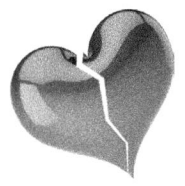

Introduction

Is your most important relationship a continuous source of joy and mutual support, or is it in danger of degenerating into apathy or becoming a battleground?

If you have heard yourself say these things in the privacy of your own mind—or even aloud—

"We just can't seem to communicate."

"Our relationship just isn't exciting anymore."

"I know I love (him/her) but our relationship has changed!"

"I could just wring (his/her) neck for forgetting..."

"I'm just not in love anymore."

"Darn, just when things were going so well, s/he got involved in a new project, and spending time with me just isn't important

to him/her right now. By the time s/he comes back, I may be too angry to care."

"I love being in love, but it just doesn't last. I keep wishing my relationship would be romantic forever."

"I thought s/he was just great at first, but I never dreamed s/he would try so hard to control everything."

Then, just spend an hour a week following the suggestions in this little book and create the joyful, supportive, loving relationship you long for. Isn't your relationship worth it?

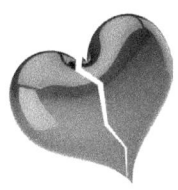

Part 1
The Challenge: Keep Your Relationship Vibrant and Growing

You Want to Be Close

People often feel angry, sad or confused because they believe a life partner is treating them badly, but what I've seen is that they have let accumulated small resentments build walls between them, when all they really want is to be close to each other.

Sometimes when on the surface your relationship with your life partner seems to be serene, you know in your heart there is something difficult, deep or challenging you want to say, but you're afraid to rock the boat by saying it. You fear that either you or your partner will not feel heard, seen or understood by each other.

You're Uncomfortable Talking About Problems

You may believe that never arguing with each other will make your relationship strong. What usually happens though, is because you're both human, you have different needs and wants. If you pretend your needs and wants don't exist and don't ask your partner to consider them, you feel disappointed and angry.

You may think that you must give up some part of yourself to be in a relationship or that you have to give up the relationship in order to be yourself. But what I've seen is when we give up trying to please our partners at all costs, we have a lot more room to be ourselves.

When you avoid the difficult conversations about your feelings and hide them instead of risking an argument, the pressure of those hidden feelings builds up. It leads you to conclude that the relationship is not right for you, and you sometimes think your only option is to leave.

You Do Have to Do Some Work

The fantasy is that if a relationship is right, you won't have to work at it. The truth is that even though there is work involved in keeping a relationship healthy, most people agree it's worth a little investment of energy for the payoff of having an incredible sense of connection to their partner.

The key to experiencing the joy that comes with this incredible level of connection is being able to have the right kind of conversations with your partner. What I've seen is when people learn to argue in healthy ways, they tend to stay together. And with a few tools, these difficult conversations not only get easier, they also become amazing opportunities for solving problems and creating great relationships.

Is This the Relationship You're Dreaming About?

In great relationships:

- You share your dreams.
- You talk together about what is important to each of you, even if you disagree.
- You hear each other out without feeling threatened.
- You affirm each other's right to be different and still be together.
- You appreciate how your differences contribute to the richness of your relationship.

When you encounter problems:

- You focus on the outcomes you want and how to achieve them instead of fighting about whose solution is right.
- You are realistic about money and other resources and together make appropriate choices about how to use them.

Being Happy Together

- You creatively develop the resources to have fun together and
- achieve your dreams.
- You create time and space to do what you both love to do, remembering what drew you together in the first place.
- You create time and space for each of you to do what you love to do alone.
- You love the times you're outrageous and/or silly together.
- You freely admit your vulnerabilities to each other and help each other without depleting yourselves.
- You allow each other space to be yourselves and willingly risk helping each other grow and change as you evolve together and separately.
- When you encounter challenges that seem overwhelming, you find and use outside resources

> to help you move forward on your life journey together.

In a great relationship you and your partner empower each other, and the relationship becomes powerful, exciting, playful, nurturing and creative. You feel excited, safe and loved.

When you and your partner both want to develop a great relationship, the journey is wonderfully exciting and joyful.

Even when only one partner holds the image of what it's possible to create in a relationship while the other thinks that things are good enough the way they are, don't despair. Many people undertake the beginning of this journey alone and break ground for their partners, who are encouraged by the progress they see and come along a little later.

The Right Conversations Make the Difference

If you are going to have a great connection with your partner—you need to be able to have the right kind of conversation, one that lets both parties feel heard, seen and understood.

The skills you need to have these conversations include the ability to bring both your own and your partner's needs, strengths, values and limitations to the table in each and every conversation.

The instructions you find in this book will help you develop the skills to understand each other, even if you disagree, and to creatively use your combined knowledge and intuition to find resources to satisfy both of you.

When you understand what you want, what you are good at, and what you can and can't control, you'll learn to stop focusing on what is wrong with your partner and instead see what your partner can actually do to make you happy.

If what you want is to feel close to your life partner, to find the happiness you've dreamed about, instead of giving up because it's gotten hard, you probably need to learn the art of having important conversations. Then you can both give each other the gift of being heard, seen and understood.

Relationships are a Work in Progress

If you want to know more about how normal relationships develop, read the next part. If you are more interested in the "how to," just skip past it and start having your conversations.

Relationships Evolve or Die

Relationships do change—and in predictable ways. The better you understand the pattern, the better equipped you will be to help your most valued relationships grow and develop into mature, sustaining supports for you. Relationships that do not continuously develop tend to either stagnate or die.

Developing relationships cycle through five different stages. Stages of adult relationships mirror the relationships you experienced as a child with the important adults who cared for you.

Being Happy Together

1. Bonding (also known as falling in love or temporary insanity).

2. Co-dependency (two become one or I'll take care of you if you take care of me).

3. Power struggle (I don't like this co-dependency any more or I'm right and you're wrong).

4. Independence (two separate people who no longer need each other).

5. Interdependence (maturity: two independent people who care for and respect each other).

Relationships can move from stage one to stage five in a few hours, a few months or a few years, or they can get stuck in the co-dependency or power struggle stages and stay there for a lifetime.

Even mature relationships with life partners tend to recycle through stages two through five as life circumstances (moving to a new city, having a baby, etc.) change. People often end relationships at stage three and seek new relationships in order to reexperience stage one.

Here's how it happens.

Falling in Love

Stage one, bonding, is about DNA reproducing itself. It is the biological purpose of your genes to survive and reproduce. Personalities don't really matter. It is distressingly temporary and lasts just about long enough to get babies started.

Stage one feels blissful. It's so blissful that for some people it becomes addictive. It is the stage of parents gazing at their new infant with awe and adoration. It is also the stage of lovers gazing at each other the same way. It is the stage of "You're my BEST friend!" It is the honeymoon phase of your relationship.

It is the time of rose-colored glasses. We see only the best in each other. Often, we don't really see each other at all.

Instead, we see only a reflection of our own hopes and dreams.

Relationship development advice for stage one: Expect to "fall out of love" with your partner (or your new friend, or your new job). Being "in love" is temporary insanity that lasts long enough for nature to get babies (or new projects) started. A mature loving relationship is better and takes time to develop.

You Make Me Whole

Stage two, co-dependency, is the experience of being completed by another person. It is the persistent cultural myth of two people becoming one.

What that really means is two whole people each believe that they must ignore important parts of themselves and act as if they are half people in order to merge into one whole person.

They usually divide up the chores of personhood. One may take the role of the thinker; the other previously competent person rarely thinks within the relationship but feels enough feelings for both of them. One may become the caretaker and the other the one who needs care.

This is an appropriate relationship for a parent and a very small child who really is not yet competent to care for him/herself.

It is very common in a traditional relationship with an authoritarian structure. The husband is "supposed to" think and the wife is "supposed to" do what is expected of her.

It rarely works out that way, and it leads to much unhappiness.

It is a basically unstable relationship, because both partners are more than their roles in the relationship. Those other feelings and abilities that are not supposed to be expressed keep showing up and causing problems.

Actually, those other qualities are an expression of an unquenchable human spirit.

Relationship development advice for stage two: Keep your individuality while building your relationship. Two becoming one is an outmoded notion—it really means that each of you becomes half the person you were and is guaranteed to lead to resentment. (So does abandoning who you are in order to keep a job).

It's All Your Fault

Stage three, the power struggle, occurs when either person in the relationship gets tired of trying to be only a half-person and starts to assert her/himself and protest the arrangement. It can get especially ugly when the other person tries to maintain the status quo.

The prototype of this battle is the healthy two-year-old discovering and demonstrating to her/his parents that s/he is indeed a separate person.

The power struggle can be about almost anything—how to do a job, whether to keep time agreements, who is in charge of what, what is the right way to do things or how did something really happen. It is really about asserting (reasserting) individuality. The operant phrase is "You're not the boss of me!"

The battle can also go underground with passive-aggressive behavior that is both frustrating and bewildering.

Relationship development advice for stage three: Change the behavior in yourself that you don't like in your partner. It is all too easy to ignore things you don't like about yourself, and instead, pay attention to how annoyed you are that your partner does those very same things. This is called projection.

I Don't Need You Anymore ... Now What?

Stage four, independence, comes when you both realize that neither of you is going to change the other. You give up trying to make your partner do things your way and start to create your own life. You accept the responsibility and authority you need to live your own life and get on with doing it. After all the struggles, most people experience this stage with great relief.

The discomfort in this stage comes when something seems to be missing. If you no longer need each other, why stay together?

You are so interested in self-discovery that others may see you as self-centered. This can be a time when you may drift apart, or as lovers, you discover that you can become friends too.

This period of developing self-awareness is a necessary prelude to creating a rich, mature relationship.

Relationship development advice for stage four: Do whatever makes you feel vibrant and alive, even if you need to do it alone. When you feel vibrant and alive, you are attractive to your partner and to others.

We Made It!

Stage five, interdependence, is a mature, synergistic relationship. You are two independent people who, together, are more than the sum of your individual selves. You create magic together.

You share values together, you solve problems together, you can play together, and you can nurture each other appropriately. You each have outside interests that contribute to the larger community and enhance your relationship with each other. You understand and accept each other's faults and limitations and appreciate each other's value.

Relationship development advice for stage five: Spend time working on your relationship as well as living in the relationship. Good relationships don't just happen—they need to be cultivated, watered and weeded, just like a garden.

Keeping Your Relationship Alive and Flourishing

Relationships bring incredible richness to our lives. Notice where you are in your own relationship. You may even be in more than one stage at the same time. You may be co-dependent about food, in a power struggle about household responsibilities, and independent about money all at the same time.

If you want your relationship to grow, focus on what you need to do to help it develop to the next stage, and do it.

The rest of this book is about what you can do in less than an hour every week to create the warm, loving relationship most people only dream about.

Use This Program Your Own Way

Just reading this book will not create the relationship of your dreams. You must take action. In fact, you must take lots of actions. Plan to spend some time on this project. You and your relationship are worth it.

This book is like a buffet, and this buffet contains 125 items. If you chose one item a week, you have enough to last you well over two years. And just because you do an activity once does not mean it is used up. You can go back to whatever works for you.

There is no right way to eat at a buffet. When you go, you probably look over the banquet and choose the items that appeal to you. You rarely eat everything available. Use the rest of this book the same way.

Page through it and stop to read the sections that seem most relevant to you. Invite your partner to look it over too. Choose the activities that seem most relevant to either or both of you.

Or ...

Do it your own way. Invent something that works for you and send me an email to tell me about it.

LaurieWeiss@EmpowermentSystems.com

Just do it!

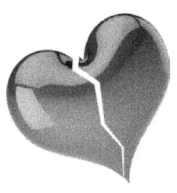

Part 2

About Relationships

Myths about relationships can make you miserable.

Following these suggestions relieves the pressure and

helps you create the relationship you deserve.

Chapter 1
It's OK to Be Different

Expect differences. We tend to choose relationships because our partner is different, and then spend all our time trying to get him/her to change and be exactly like us.

A part of you is both attracted and scared by your partner's differentness. A stable person initially loves the excitement created by a more adventurous partner but then gets worried about the long-term effects of the adventurous behavior. The adventurous one needs the stability but feels controlled and resentful because of it. Other examples of opposite, complementary traits are everywhere.

****

Your weekly assignment, should you choose to accept it:

Remember why you loved the trait you keep trying to change in your partner. Think about why that trait scares you now and about how it contributes to your relationship. Talk to each other about what you appreciate and about what you fear.

Chapter 2
Your Partner Is Your Mirror

Change the behavior in yourself that you don't like in your partner. It is all too easy to ignore things you don't like about yourself, and instead, pay attention to how annoyed you are that your partner does those very same things. This is called projection.

We all have blind spots, things we don't know about ourselves that others know about us. Use what irritates you about someone else's behavior to help you discover your own blind spots, take pressure off your partner, and decide what to do next.

****

Your weekly assignment, should you choose to accept it:

Make a list of things that irritate you when your partner does them. Take an honest look at your own behavior and see how you, too, do some of those things. Choose one thing that you intend to change about yourself and tell your partner what it is.

Chapter 3
Go Away, Closer

Expect the closeness and distance you experience with your partner to vary from hour to hour, day to day, and season to season. People experience enough closeness much as they experience enough food—any more leads to discomfort. We all have different capacities.

This dance may seem frustrating at times. You want to be close and move toward partner; your partner wants to be distant and moves away from you. It's hard not to take it personally. Talking about what you need makes it easier to accommodate to one another.

****

Your weekly assignment, should you choose to accept it:

When you seem to be out of step with each other, talk about it. If you want closeness and your partner seems withdrawn, ask specifically for what you want. S/he may be willing to sit close to you for fifteen minutes even if s/he feels the need for private space and time.

Chapter 4
Childhood Experiences Make a Difference

Understand that the experiences you had as children influence how you respond to each other now. Barely remembered traumatic events may make you or your partner hypersensitive to events that someone else would consider trivial.

When your immediate reaction to your partner's upset (often anger) is "But I didn't do anything wrong!" you probably didn't. Try responding with, "I'm sorry, I didn't mean to upset you. Can you tell me what part of what I did caused the problem?"

****

Your weekly assignment, should you choose to accept it:

Review a past upset from this perspective and try to sort out what really upset your partner. You can even ask how your behavior reminds him/her of something from the past. Ask your partner how to manage similar situations in the future.

Chapter 5
You're Both Right

Accept that differences are just that—differences. When you take the position that you are right, and your partner is wrong, nobody wins.

Often partners are attracted to each other because of their differences. A stable person and an impulsive one are drawn to each other, hoping the relationship will help each of them feel complete. Then they criticize each other for the traits that attracted them in the first place.

****

Your weekly assignment, should you choose to accept it:

List three ways in which you wish your partner were more like you. Now think about how you were attracted to at least one of those differences when your relationship was new. Tell each other why you originally liked the very thing that distresses you now.

Chapter 6
Give In—Sometimes

Vary your responses. Don't expect to always give in or to always have it your own way. Getting stuck in any position drains the energy from a relationship.

If one of you usually lets the other have his/her own way in a disagreement, the one who loses will come to resent the situation. The one who wins may be unhappy because it feels like s/he is communicating with a doormat. When you disagree, engage with each other until you fully resolve the issue. This can mean you agree to disagree.

****

Your weekly assignment, should you choose to accept it:

Look at some of your recent disagreements and see if there's a pattern where one of you is a winner in the other a loser. Choose one recent disagreement and revisit it. Each of you state your own reasons for your position, listen to your partner's reasons and either reaffirm the old decision or make a new one.

Chapter 7
Notice What Works

Learn from your experience. Notice what works and what usually receives a negative reaction from your partner. Do what works and stop doing what does not work.

Life would be so much easier if your partner would do things the way you want them done. You may want to have early morning discussions, but if the response you always get from your partner is incoherent mumbles, try another tactic. It is important to accommodate each other's preferences.

****

Your weekly assignment, should you choose to accept it:

List three things that you repeatedly do with your partner that don't get you the response you want. Think about a time in the past when you did get a response that you liked. Use that information to design a new, more effective way to get positive responses from your partner.

Chapter 8
Recovering from Temporary Insanity

Expect to fall out of love with your partner. Being in love is temporary insanity that lasts long enough for nature to get babies started. A mature loving relationship is better and takes time to develop.

When you are "in love," all you pay attention to are the things you want to see, and wish were true about each other. Reality is an unwelcome intrusion. In a mature loving relationship, you accept reality and can still play together, solve problems together, share values together and nurture each other appropriately.

* * * * * * * * * * * * *

Your weekly assignment, should you choose to accept it:

Each of you list the ways in which you play, solve problems, share values and nurture your partner. Compare your lists and decide if you want to make any changes.

Chapter 9
Your Relationship Is Worth the Challenge

Create a mature, loving relationship by using the ideas in this book. Loving relationships do not just happen. Creating them is a rewarding and worthwhile challenge.

In a mature loving relationship, you can easily discuss values, solve problems, have fun together and nurture and support each other. You and your partner empower each other and the relationship becomes powerful, exciting, playful, nurturing and creative. You feel excited, safe and loved.

****

Your weekly assignment, should you choose to accept it:

Each of you separately list times when you have discussed values, solved problems together, had fun together, and nurtured or supported each other. Compare your lists. If you had trouble coming up with examples in any area, discuss ways in which you might try some new things together to fill up the empty category.

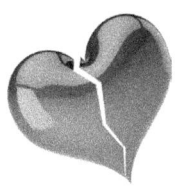

Part 3
Communication

Communication is the key to dismantling the walls that keep you apart.

Chapter 10
Courtesy Counts

Be courteous. Your partner deserves the same respectful communication you would give a stranger or a business associate.

Life partners see each other at their worst and often disappoint each other. Feeling angry is a natural response to disappointment. Acting angry toward your partner rarely accomplishes anything useful. A courteous request for change is more effective.

****

Your weekly assignment, should you choose to accept it:

Ask your partner to change a behavior that bothers you as if you were asking a very important guest to make that same change.

Chapter 11
Give Up Mind Reading

Ask your partner for what you want. Contrary to popular belief, your partner cannot and should not read your mind. Asking increases the odds of getting what you want. Be specific.

Mind reading is an inexact science. Imagine going into a restaurant and telling the server "Guess what I want to eat—and if you don't get it right, it means you don't really love me!" Your partner may be more accurate than the server in guessing what you want, but it really makes no sense to get angry, as many people do, when their partners guess incorrectly.

****

Your weekly assignment, should you choose to accept it:

Using the words, "Will you please...," ask your partner to do something for you. Asking in this way makes it possible for your partner to say yes, no or maybe in response to your request. You don't have to get everything you ask for, but it's nice to get a response.

Chapter 12
Instead of Pretending ...

Tell the truth about what you do and do not like or want. Trying to be agreeable when you really do not agree leads to confusion and resentment.

If you have been pretending that you love your partner's favorite kind of music, and you really must grit your teeth to listen to it, this would be a good time to gently talk about your own preference. If you have been going out with friends when you would rather stay home and read a book, it's time to explain to your partner that you have been trying to be agreeable.

****

Your weekly assignment, should you choose to accept it:

Choose a situation in which one of you has been being agreeable without really agreeing. Explore ways to manage that situation. You might decide to take turns doing together what only one of you really wants to do or to spend some time each following your own agenda. Look for your own creative solutions.

Chapter 13
Clarity Is Powerful

Use a rating system to let your partner know how strongly you like or dislike something. Knowing whether something is a one or a ten makes it easier for your partner to decide how to respond to you.

Often partners who try to please each other find themselves doing things that are not very exciting to either of them. A suggestion like "let's go to the mall" may be taken as a burning desire of one partner and a command performance to the other. If they investigated the situation more thoroughly, they might discover that they would each prefer to go for a walk.

****

Your weekly assignment, should you choose to accept it:

Each of you list ten things that you would like to have, do or be. Rank each item on the list on a scale of one to ten, or as extremely important, moderately important, or somewhat interesting. Share your lists with each other.

Chapter 14
Don't Say Yes, Say Maybe

Say "Maybe" when you are not sure about something. Give a time when you will provide an answer and keep your commitment.

When your partner is enthusiastic about something, you may feel pressured to make a commitment to do something before you are fully ready to do so. You need to take time to explore own thoughts and feelings before you say yes, no or offer another alternative.

****

Your weekly assignment, should you choose to accept it:

Each of you think of a time when you made a decision before you were ready. Share those memories with each other and explore whether either of you really intends to pressure the other.

Chapter 15
Remember to Say "Thanks"

Express your appreciation when your partner does something that pleases you. People love being acknowledged, and behavior that is acknowledged is usually repeated.

It's easy to forget to say "Thank you" for the little things. Many people have discovered, however, that the more frequently they pay attention to what goes right, the less frequently things seem to go wrong.

****

Your weekly assignment, should you choose to accept it:

Put ten pennies in a pocket. Every time you acknowledge your partner, switch one penny to a different pocket. Your objective is to move all your pennies from one pocket to another every day.

Chapter 16
Keep Your Agreements

Keep agreements you make with your partner. Keeping agreements builds trust, which is the basis of almost everything important.

Sometimes agreements are explicit. "I will be home at 6 PM." Sometimes they are unspoken—you each tell the other when you spend an unusual amount of money. Tell your partner in advance if you intend to change any kind of agreement.

****

Your weekly assignment, should you choose to accept it:

Remember a time when you didn't keep an agreement with your partner. Ask your partner if s/he noticed the broken agreement. Talk about what you each felt and thought in that situation.

Chapter 17
It's OK to Renegotiate

Renegotiate any agreements that you find you can't (or don't want to) keep. If you intend to change an agreement, let your partner know at the earliest opportunity, even if you feel uncomfortable about doing so.

If you're procrastinating about keeping an agreement, that may be a signal that you have overextended yourself or made an agreement that you don't want to keep. If you tell your partner now, you may be pleasantly surprised that s/he is relieved and willing to consider another way to solve the problem.

* * * * * * * * * * * * *

Your weekly assignment, should you choose to accept it:

Each of you make a list of agreements you have with your partner that you have not kept. Now make a list of agreements your partner has made with you but has not completed. Exchange lists. Are there any surprises? Renegotiate at least one agreement.

Chapter 18
Describe Your Own Emotions

Use feeling words like sad, mad, glad and scared to describe emotions. Saying "I feel (sad or glad) ..." is better than saying "I feel THAT YOU ..." Once you say the phrase "that you," you stop describing feelings and switch to a judgment you are about to lay on your partner.

You can say, "I feel scared when you [drive so fast]." Replace the specific words and action descriptions with words that fit your own situation. Notice how differently you react when your partner acknowledges his/her own feelings.

****

Your weekly assignment, should you choose to accept it:

Practice filling in the blanks: I feel (emotion) when you (an action). Start the conversation by each of you completing the sentence using the word "happy" as the emotion word.

Chapter 19
Get Permission First

Ask if your partner has time to listen to a long story before launching into it. It also helps to tell your partner, in advance, why you are telling the story. Then s/he can prepare appropriate sympathy, suggestions or questions while listening to you.

It's easy to get so involved with your own need to have someone hear you that you forget about your partner's agenda. Always consider both your own needs and your partner's needs in any situation.

****

Your weekly assignment, should you choose to accept it:

Think about what you would like your partner to say or do after s/he has heard your story. Say "I would like to tell you about (your topic), and I would like you to (whatever you want your partner to say or do) when I finish. Is this a good time?"

Chapter 20

Listen, Listen, Listen

Listen carefully to what your partner says. Ask direct questions until you really understand what your partner is telling you. Attentive listening is often the greatest gift you can give another person.

We're often so busy that we barely listen to each other. When we do listen, we're so busy figuring out what we will need to do about what's being said or how we are going to respond, that we listen very selectively.

★★★★★★★★★★★★

Your weekly assignment, should you choose to accept it:

Take two twenty-minute time periods where you can practice attentively listening to each other. When your partner is speaking, don't interrupt unless you don't understand what's being said. Ask questions only for clarification and listen to the answers. After your partner finishes speaking, wait at least five seconds before responding.

Chapter 21
Slow Down to Match Your Partner

Allow your partner time to think about the answer to your question and to answer at his/her own speed. Leaving a few seconds of quiet may seem uncomfortable at first but may allow time for important thoughts to surface and be expressed.

Partners often operate at different speeds, and the faster one may become impatient and assume that the slower one isn't paying attention or doesn't care about the answer. The slower one may even find it useful to say, "I need time to think about it, and I will answer (at a specific time)."

****

Your weekly assignment, should you choose to accept it:

Have a conversation about whether either of you feels pressured to answer the other instead of having time to really check your own thoughts and feelings before responding. If this is a problem for you, practice following the suggestions above.

Chapter 22

Ask Before You Try to Help

Find out whether your partner wants your help in solving a problem before you jump in and offer suggestions. Some people just want a sympathetic listener and will feel insulted if you try to help.

It's only natural to want to help solve a problem. However, we don't always know what will be the best help we could give our partner. Try asking, "What can I do help?" Listen to the answer, and then decide what to offer.

****

Your weekly assignment, should you choose to accept it:

Practice asking your partner, "What can I do help?" When your partner asks you that question, be sure it is answered thoughtfully instead of automatically.

Chapter 23
Find Out What's Really Needed

(This one is so important, I found two different ways to say it! LW.)

Ask what kind of help your partner wants before taking action. Your partner may surprise you by asking you to do something you would not think of on your own.

When you jump in to solve your partner's problem without asking first, you often do the wrong thing. Your partner may then feel angry because all s/he wanted was sympathy or a chance to clarify his/her own thoughts. Asking, "How can I help?" is a good way to start the conversation.

****

Your weekly assignment, should you choose to accept it:

Talk with each other about whether you usually get the kind of help you need when you have a problem. Decide whether being asked, "How can I help?" would be useful for you.

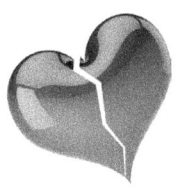

Part 4
Difficult Communication

With a few tools, difficult conversations not only get easier, they also become amazing opportunities for solving problems and creating great relationships.

Chapter 24
Don't Delay; Talk About It—Now

Discuss problems as soon as your recognize their existence. Don't pretend things are OK when they are not. Resentments that build up over time are harder to manage than the original problem.

You may think something isn't important enough to talk about, or you may hope that the problem will go away by itself. It usually doesn't. You may even be afraid of what your partner will do if you bring it up. Take the risk of talking about it calmly. Ask your partner to help figure out a solution to the problem that will work for both of you.

****

Your weekly assignment, should you choose to accept it:

Think about something that has been bothering you that you don't re-ally want to share with your partner. Imagine the worst thing that could possibly happen if you shared it. Decide whether you want to risk that outcome. If you're willing to take the risk, share what's bothering you with your partner. If you're not willing to take the risk, it might be useful to discuss the problem with a trusted friend or advisor.

Chapter 25
Anger Means You Want Something to Be Different

Figure out what you want your partner to do differently when you are angry and communicate specifically what s/he can do to satisfy you. Most people don't want to hear about anger, because they think there is nothing they can do to fix it.

You're usually angry at your partner because s/he has caused a problem for you. Would you still be angry if the problem went away? Ask your partner to do whatever it takes to fix the problem.

****

Your weekly assignment, should you choose to accept it:

Think about something your partner did or did not do that caused you a problem and that you are angry about. Can s/he fix the problem now? If so, tell your partner specifically what you would like to have done to make your anger disappear. Ask if s/he will do that within a specific time. If it's impossible to still fix the problem, think of a list of favors your partner could do for you to make amends for creating the problem. Negotiate to trade your anger for a favor that would make your life easier or more pleasant now.

Chapter 26
Give Advance Warning of Unilateral Changes

Warn your partner when you are about to change the rules and do things differently. If you have always hung up the clothes s/he left around, say that you will no longer do that task.

Over time, you and your partner create expectations of each other without ever putting them into words. When expectations are not met, people often feel uneasy and angry. Advance warning makes it easier to accept changes.

****

Your weekly assignment, should you choose to accept it:

Make a list of three things you do now that you would like to change. Choose the one you think will affect your partner the least. Explain what you intend to change and make the change within 24 hours.

Chapter 27
Break a Vicious Cycle

Speak in sentences or, at most, paragraphs instead of pages during a difficult conversation. Your partner will only remember the last sentence or two you say and forget the beginning of a long speech.

It's paradoxical! The more you want to be certain you are understood, the more you talk to make sure you've said everything. The more you talk without pausing, the less feedback you get. The less feedback you get, the more worried you are that you are not being understood, and so you continue to talk, others stop listening, and you create the result you fear.

****

Your weekly assignment, should you choose to accept it:

Have a conversation with your partner. Take turns, each of you saying no more than three sentences at a time. This is more interesting if you choose a "hot topic" on which you disagree.

Chapter 28
Prove That You're Listening

Paraphrase your partner's words when you are having a difficult conversation and ask if you understood the words correctly. Just saying "I understand" is usually not telling the truth: you probably don't.

Tell your partner what you think they just told you, using your own words. Be sure to include a description of the emotion your partner seems to be expressing. "You are feeling sad because ..." Ask your partner "Did I get that right?" If the answer is no, try again. If the answer is yes, continue the conversation.

****

Your weekly assignment, should you choose to accept it:

Practice this technique on an important conversation until you are comfortable using it. It does slow down the conversation—a useful thing to do during an argument.

Chapter 29
Speak After You Listen

(This point is just a little bit different than the last one. Practice both. LW.)

Add your own thoughts to the conversation only after your partner acknowledges that you understand. This slows down a difficult conversation and makes it less likely that you will say things that you will later regret.

In a heated discussion, you probably want to be certain that your partner understands your point of view. You may even be ready to explain it at length. Instead, listen carefully to your partner and share your understanding of what your partner has just communicated. When you are finished, ask, "Is that what you mean?" When your partner says yes, then, and only then, share your position.

****

Your weekly assignment, should you choose to accept it:

Learn this skill before you need to use it in a "hot" conversation. Practice telling your partner your understanding of what he/she has shared with you. Then ask whether you understood correctly. Then make YOUR own point. Make sure each one of you gets a turn in each position.

Chapter 30
Face-to-Face May Be Too Close

Create conversations by phone, text or email instead of face-to-face when you keep getting stuck in the same old patterns. It is often easier to stick to discussing information when you can't react to the expressions on each other's faces.

Conversing this way is especially useful when you are angry at each other and must resolve something anyhow. If you are using text or email, count to ten and reread what you have written before hitting the send button.

****

Your weekly assignment, should you choose to accept it:

Choose a problem you have not been able to resolve together. Set aside time to have a telephone, text or email conversation focused on the problem. After the conversation, discuss whether the technique works for you.

Chapter 31
Careful Confrontation Works — Here's How

Confront behavior you consider dangerous or destructive. Describe your own feelings about the situation. "I feel scared when the car moves this fast," instead of, "You're driving too fast."

It's natural to try to control a situation to protect either or both of you from danger. Unfortunately, trying to control (you're driving) invites anger and resistance. Showing your vulnerability (I feel scared) often encourages your partner to take care of you by changing his/her behavior.

****

Your weekly assignment, should you choose to accept it:

Remember a time when each of you felt angry about your partner telling you what to do. Think of something s/he could have done differently in that situation. Share your insights with each other.

Chapter 32
Request Behavior Changes

Request that your partner change behavior that causes you a problem. If you ask for what you want, you are more likely (but not certain) to get it than if you keep quiet and stay annoyed.

Your partner is more likely to be receptive to your request if you describe the impact of his/her current behavior on you now and how the change will make your life easier. Your complaint needs to be followed by a specific request to do something differently. Instead of "Let me know if you'll be late," try, "Call me as soon as you know you will be more than ten minutes late and let me know what time you expect to arrive."

****

Your weekly assignment, should you choose to accept it:

Think of something your partner does or does not do that you have been tolerating because it doesn't seem important enough to mention or complain about. This should be something that really does annoy you. Tell your partner, "This is a small annoyance for me that I hope you will consider changing. Whenever I (find your dirty dishes in the living room), I feel (irritated, frustrated) ..., because I (really hate a messy house). In the future, will you please (put them into the dishwasher yourself)?" Negotiate if necessary.

Chapter 33
Let Your Partner Be Right

Explain how a change you are requesting will solve a problem for you without implying that s/he is wrong or bad for doing what upsets you. After all, s/he may honestly believe that making beds is a waste of time.

Your partner may see no logical reason to make a change you are requesting. However, s/he might be willing to make the change when you explain how it will make your life easier, whether it's logical or not.

****

Your weekly assignment, should you choose to accept it:

Each of you list several changes you would like your partner to make. Think about the most important reason you want that change made. Each of you request that the other make one change and explain the reasons for your request. This is not a guarantee that your partner will make the change, but it could be the start of the negotiation.

Chapter 34
Deliberately Create Consequences

Decide what you will do when your partner persists in behavior you have requested that s/he change. Tell your partner about your decision. The next time it happens, do what you said you would do—even if you are scared.

It's easier to start this behavior when you need to address a minor problem. If your partner clutters your mutual space and you are tired of the mess, tell your partner you will take the clutter and put it in a box in the basement. Then do it. When your partner asks, "Where is my___?" just say exactly what you did with it.

****

Your weekly assignment, should you choose to accept it:

Have a conversation about something each one of you has agreed to do or change, but not followed through in your agreement. Decide together on a creative consequence that will occur next time your partner notices the offending behavior.

Chapter 35
Respond Instead of Counterattacking

Admit your mistakes even if you don't like the way your partner confronts you about them. It is tempting to defend yourself by attacking your partner, but if you do, you both lose in the long run.

When you feel attacked by your partner's tone of voice or angry expression, it's much easier to think about what s/he is doing wrong instead of what's being said. Make the effort to listen and respond to your partner's words. You can discuss your feelings about the delivery system later.

****

Your weekly assignment, should you choose to accept it:

Discuss a recent situation in which either you or your partner was unhappy about the outcome. Practice acknowledging to each other what you did that made the situation worse. It can be as simple as saying, "Yes, I raised my voice."

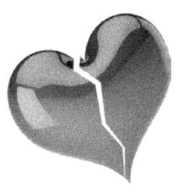

Part 5
Play

It's way too easy to get so involved in
your responsibilities that you forget to play —
but isn't play what attracted you to each other
in the first place?

Chapter 36

Being Silly Is Good for You

Play together in silly ways. Blow bubbles, finger paint with chocolate pudding on the kitchen table and lick it off, splash each other, sing ...

When you are tired, stressed or tense, one of the fastest ways to release the tension is to find a reason to laugh together. Doing silly things together is a great way to do this. It doesn't have to take very long, and either one of you can start the process rolling.

****

Your weekly assignment, should you choose to accept it:

Make a list of silly things you can do together. Choose one thing and do it. If you can't think of anything to put on your list, choose something from my earlier suggestions and do that.

Chapter 37
Touching Is Connecting

Enjoy touching each other in both sexual and nonsexual ways. Enjoy is the important word—it means you must communicate about what is pleasurable and what is not.

Being physically touched is the very first way every human being learns that s/he is important, so touch is an extremely powerful communication tool. You each have your own history about what kind of touch has been most pleasurable to you. Your partner may not even suspect what you want most, unless you talk about it.

****

Your weekly assignment, should you choose to accept it:

Have a conversation with your partner and learn what kind of touch (location, how light or firm, timing, lights on or off, etc.) s/he likes most. Then practice doing it.

Chapter 38
Laugh With Each Other

Laugh together. Share the jokes or cartoons that make you grin, watch a funny video or remember the stories about funny (especially in retrospect) things you have experienced together.

Laughter is healing and brings you closer together. It's a great way of relieving tension, especially about the unavoidable challenges of living in such a complex world.

****

Your weekly assignment, should you choose to accept it:

Whenever something makes you smile or laugh this week, take a moment and share it with your partner.

BEING HAPPY TOGETHER

Chapter 39
Expand Your Play Horizons

Schedule time to play together. Keep a list of activities you each consider fun. Take turns choosing an item from the list and do it.

When you aren't used to playing, it's sometimes hard to figure out what you want to do when you have time to do it. Take time to make this list before you are ready to use it. Include activities that each one of you enjoys separately, activities you think you might enjoy, and activities you have enjoyed together in the past.

****

Your weekly assignment, should you choose to accept it:

Take the time to make your list. Start by making separate lists, and then brainstorm together about other items you could add to the list. Don't worry about cost or feasibility. Having outrageous items on your list creates interesting possibilities.

Chapter 40

Go Out to Play Together

Walk, hike or plant flowers together. Being outdoors, even to do "work," makes most people feel happy.

When we're indoors, there are constant reminders of many things we need to do. These may distract us from being together. Getting away from those reminders, even for a little while, reminds us of going out to play when we were children.

****

Your weekly assignment, should you choose to accept it:

When you're both busy being responsible and doing what needs to be done, suggest a break. Invite your partner to take a walk with you. Play hooky and enjoy yourselves.

Chapter 41
A Mini-vacation? Just Do It

Take a mini-vacation. Go away for the weekend, or for an hour or two, with minimal planning, just because it seems like a good idea.

Spontaneity is a wonderful way of keeping your relationship fresh. The more often you act spontaneously, the more likely you are to do so again. Be sure to take time to do what you want to do as well as to follow through on all your commitments.

* * * * * * * * * * * *

Your weekly assignment, should you choose to accept it:

Decide what you want to do, and Just Do It!

Chapter 42
Take the Initiative Yourself

Organize the activities you are most interested in doing. If your partner agrees to accompany you to a concert or sporting event you particularly want to attend, you get the tickets.

Most people feel a bit resentful when they are expected to take initiative to manage someone else's priority. Sometimes they procrastinate until all the good seats are gone. Avoid disappointment by taking responsibility for getting exactly what you want.

****

Your weekly assignment, should you choose to accept it:

Review the entertainment section of the newspaper and invite your partner to join you at an event you would especially enjoy. If s/he says yes, you arrange the tickets. If s/he says no, make arrangements to go alone or with a friend.

Chapter 43
What a Strange Way to Solve a Problem

Challenge your partner to resolve a problem with a squirt bottle duel at ten paces. If the situation is extremely serious, try aerosol whipped cream (at three paces) instead.

Your lives may be so busy and focused that you forget to play with each other. Doing something that is totally absurd changes the energy of any situation.

****

Your weekly assignment, should you choose to accept it:

Go shopping for squirt bottles. Decorate them with permanent markers. Practice dueling.

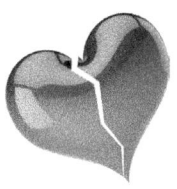

Part 6

Tasks

Doing stuff takes a big chunk out of your time.

Make the doing as stress-free as you possibly can.

Chapter 44

Negotiate and Renegotiate

Negotiate about tasks. Avoid sex-role stereotypes. Divide chores based on individual preferences and skills.

You may discover that a task you dislike and thought you needed to do is something your partner doesn't mind doing at all. One couple discovered that she loved to cut the grass and he enjoyed quiet time alone while cleaning up the kitchen.

****

Your weekly assignment, should you choose to accept it:

Each of you make a list of tasks you dislike doing. Rate each item from mild dislike to hate. Share your lists and see if you can trade some of your tasks. Think about creative solutions for items you both rate as hate.

Chapter 45
Do It, Delegate It or Dump It

Hire someone to do the chores you both hate—or do them together. Start by looking at the things that never seem to get done, probably because neither of you wants to do them.

Procrastination is usually a symptom of not wanting to do something. Talk about the symptom instead of ignoring it. Imagine what would really happen if the task was never completed. Then decide what to do. Do not make promises that have been made before.

****

Your weekly assignment, should you choose to accept it:

List three chores you both hate. Either arrange for one of them to be done by someone else or do one of them together.

Chapter 46
Finish Something and Celebrate

Work together on something hard that will feel great when it's done, like removing a dead tree stump or tearing down an old fence or wall. The sense of accomplishment helps you feel connected to each other.

Something hard can also be a creative project. It could be shopping for a piece of furniture or designing a new kitchen. It could even be organizing your important papers. The important thing is that it's a finite task that you can do together and celebrate when you've completed it.

****

Your weekly assignment, should you choose to accept it:

Make a list of tasks that are challenging and that you could do together. Choose one of the tasks, and either do it or create a plan about how and when you will do it.

Chapter 47
Practice Project Management

Make clear agreements about which of you will do which parts of a complicated task, like arranging a vacation. Check each item off your joint list as it is completed. Posting the list on the bathroom mirror or the refrigerator door works well.

Keeping each other informed about progress eliminates lots of questioning and tension. It also eliminates unpleasant surprises like discovering that each one of you thought that the other was responsible for an important part of the task.

****

Your weekly assignment, should you choose to accept it:

Choose a project to work with for practice. Together, using sticky notes, make a list of all the things that need to be done to complete the project. Write each task on a separate sticky note and divide the tasks by arranging the notes into separate lists. Be creative and have fun.

Chapter 48
Keep a List

Avoid emergency shopping trips. Keep a running shopping list. The person who takes the last item from storage should note that it needs replacement.

Simple things, like running out of needed supplies, create unnecessary tension in your relationship. It is easier to set up systems to prevent problems than it is to deal with managing each small problem as it arises.

****

Your weekly assignment, should you choose to accept it:

Post a shopping list in an easily accessible place with a pen nearby. Brainstorm together about what items should be on the list right now, and start the list. Tell your partner each time you add an item to the list until keeping the list gets to be a habit for both of you.

Chapter 49
Avoid Unpleasant Surprises

Inform your partner as soon as possible if you will not be doing a task that s/he expects you to do. This avoids unpleasant surprises and lets you solve the problem of what to do about the undone task together.

Whether it's grocery shopping, making travel arrangements or even changing light bulbs, inform your partner about any potential problem before s/he learns about it accidentally.

****

Your weekly assignment, should you choose to accept it:

Discuss whether this is a problem for either of you. If it is, set up a regular time to inform each other about upcoming changes. Do this daily or weekly depending upon what you need.

Chapter 50
Do It Together

Share a routine task one of you would normally do alone. Spend the time talking together and enjoying each other's company.

It is easy to get so involved in the business of living that you forget to enjoy each other. Change the comfortable patterns occasionally in order to experience each other in new ways. Wake up and appreciate each other again.

****

Your weekly assignment, should you choose to accept it:

Invite your partner to go grocery shopping, do yard work, write the checks or cook a meal with you. Talk about what you are doing together. Share a hope or dream you have been keeping to yourself. Plan something else you can do together that you usually do alone.

Chapter 51
Surprise Your Partner

Occasionally do a task that your partner does not expect you to do. Let your partner be pleasantly surprised that s/he does not need to prepare dinner or mow the lawn.

Regular routines can numb you so much that you forget to appreciate each other. Occasionally stepping into your partner's shoes will reawaken your awareness of things you ordinarily take for granted.

****

Your weekly assignment, should you choose to accept it:

Do a task you ordinarily consider your partner's responsibility. It might be making breakfast, setting up a social engagement, washing the car or doing the laundry. Talk to each other about what you learned by doing this.

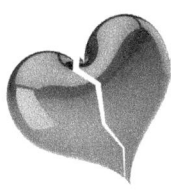

Part 7
Boundaries

"A river without banks is a swamp."

Jean Houston

When you have boundaries, you don't need to watch out for alligators.

Chapter 52
Do You Really Need Control?

Give up control of "your" kitchen if you want your partner's help. So what if you have to look for something that is not in its proper place—it probably is not very far away, and you can ask where it is if you get desperate.

Avoiding criticism is a powerful motivation to stay out of the kitchen. If your partner expects you to be upset each time s/he makes a mistake, you won't get the help that you want. Decide whether it's more important to get help or to stay in control. If you want help, you need to relax.

****

Your weekly assignment, should you choose to accept it:

Ask your partner to do a simple task in the kitchen, like emptying the dishwasher. Watch what s/he does and notice how it is different from the way you would do that task. Then notice that the task is still completed. Decide whether it's more important to have the task completed or to have the task completed exactly the way you would do it.

Chapter 53
Substitute Cooperation for Control

Give up control of your tools if you do not want to do all repairs yourself. If things get scattered, discuss boundaries that will suit both of you.

In this case, maintaining control often means not getting any help. If you want your partner's help on a project, you may have to relax a bit. Your partner may have different standards than you do for the care and maintenance of your things. Show your partner, very specifically, what you would like to have done with your things. This process could apply to electronic devices, hobby equipment, or even kitchen supplies and equipment.

****

Your weekly assignment, should you choose to accept it:

Invite your partner to tour your workshop, toolbox, kitchen cabinets, etc. Explain how you have organized your things and under what conditions your partner may use them. Ask if your partner is willing to comply with your conditions. If your conditions don't work for your partner, keep negotiating until you find something that does.

Chapter 54
You Don't Have to Share Everything

Protect what is important to you. If you have a cherished collection that is yours alone, or a private journal, or tools you use for your own work, it's fine to set clear boundaries and not allow your partner access to them.

Some people need more privacy than others. It all depends on your personality type and your family background. You may need to have a conversation and be very explicit about what things are off limits. If your partner understands why those things are private, s/he will be more likely to honor your boundaries.

****

Your weekly assignment, should you choose to accept it:

Have a conversation about what you each needed to do to protect your own possessions from others when you were a child.

Chapter 55
Respect Each Other's Privacy

Respect your partner's boundaries. If you are curious, ask why it is important to your partner to keep some particular thing private, but do not insist on seeing or using it.

People don't want to share for many different reasons. Sometimes they fear ridicule, sometimes they fear displeasing another, and sometimes they fear losing something they value. Sometimes they are hiding a surprise for you.

****

Your weekly assignment, should you choose to accept it:

Each of you identify one or two things you want to keep private. It could be your diary, your personal checkbook, your junk drawer, a box of special cookies or a project you are designing. Let each other know what you consider off limits.

Chapter 56
Being too Polite Causes Problems

Name the movie you would like to see or the restaurant you like best, before you ask your partner's preference. That way you avoid being angry because your partner did not read your mind.

If you want to eat at an Italian restaurant, say so. If you ask your partner first, s/he might suggest a steak house or a Chinese restaurant, without ever knowing your preference. If you speak first, and your partner does not like your suggestion, then s/he can suggest an alternative and you can negotiate.

****

Your weekly assignment, should you choose to accept it:

Practice stating what you want before you ask for your partner's preferences. For example, instead of asking your partner "Are you ready to go to bed?" say "I'm ready to go to bed now, are you?"

Chapter 57
Explore the Reasons for Your Preferences

Negotiate your conflicting choices by first asking the reason for your partner's preference. You may think your partner wants a certain kind of food, when s/he really likes the atmosphere or service at a particular restaurant.

People often get into trouble when they negotiate about how to solve a problem without really understanding the nature of the problem. When you discover the reason that your partner wants something, you may find that there are many different ways to satisfy that desire.

****

Your weekly assignment, should you choose to accept it:

List several areas in which you have very different preferences. Examples: rock music/jazz, skiing/surfing, fine dining/fast food and adventure movies/romantic movies. Talk with each other about why you each like what you like.

Chapter 58
Make Clear Agreements—and Change Them When Necessary

Make clear agreements about how to play with other people when you and your partner enjoy very different activities. If your partner hates the music or movies you love most, which other people is it OK for you to enjoy them with? How frequently? With how much advance notice?

Even when you agree that you do not need to do everything together, you may find yourself uncomfortable about the relationship your partner develops with his/her "activity buddies." One conversation will not be enough to resolve this. You will need to keep talking about it to keep from resenting your partner's activities.

****

Your weekly assignment, should you choose to accept it:

Have the conversation about your boundary preferences when your partner is out playing without you. HINT: If you are uncomfortable, examine the underlying cause of your discomfort, and incorporate that into a new boundary.

Chapter 59
Insulate Your Partner from Outside Negativity

Let your partner know when you are distressed instead of dumping anger that belongs to someone else into your relationship. If someone is mean to you, tell your partner instead of passing on the meanness.

When you're stewing about a difficult experience, you may be radiating negativity toward your partner. If you tell your partner what's going on s/he can be sympathetic and supportive instead of getting angry and responding to your energy.

****

Your weekly assignment, should you choose to accept it:

Talk about times that this kind of behavior has been a problem in your relationship. Set up a signal you can use when one of you notices that the other seems to be upset. Sometimes just asking "Are you angry at me?" is all it takes to start an important conversation.

Chapter 60
Make Important Decisions Together

Share the power and the decision-making. Avoid the resentment that comes when one is burdened with responsibility and the other resents being told what to do.

When it comes to decision-making, two heads really are better than one, even if one of you knows far more than the other about a particular subject. Taking the time to thoroughly explain your rationale for your decision to your partner will clarify all of the information for both of you.

****

Your weekly assignment, should you choose to accept it:

List the decisions each of you makes without input from the other. Decide which of the decisions are minor and which ones are extremely important to both of you. Review one of the important decisions together.

Chapter 61
Don't Retaliate—Period

Forgot retaliation. If you think your partner is preoccupied and ignoring you, look at the ways you are ignoring your partner and change your own behavior. This works for any behavior you don't like.

We all have our blind spots. It's lots easier to criticize others then to look at your own behavior. It's challenging to recognize that sometimes you are not doing as well as you would like to believe you are. Accept the challenge.

****

Your weekly assignment, should you choose to accept it:

Think about something your partner does that drives you crazy. Ask yourself if you do it also. If the answer is no, ask yourself why you don't do it. Share what you learn with your partner.

Chapter 62
Obedience School???

Go to obedience school training with your dog. You must learn to communicate clearly about boundaries when you work with animals.

This obviously isn't for everybody, but it's surprising how effective it is. When someone is giving you feedback about the messages you are sending to your dog, you often learn a great deal about your general communications style. When you do this together, learning to provide consistent messages to your dog, you tend to see your own patterns of inconsistencies and learn to correct them.

****

Your weekly assignment, should you choose to accept it:

Spend some time researching obedience school training classes. Your veterinarian, a local pet store and friends are all good resources.

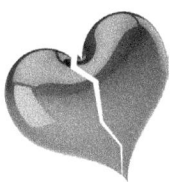

Part 8
Money

*Lack of communication about money
may not be the root of all evil in a relationship—
but it certainly comes close.*

Chapter 63
Start by Paying Attention

Talk about money. Discuss where it comes from and where it goes, and why.

Money can be a very difficult topic to discuss rationally instead of emotionally. Sometimes the very idea of talking about it makes one or both of you uncomfortable. If this is true for you, talking about money is an especially important thing to do.

****

Your weekly assignment, should you choose to accept it:

Keep track of every bit of the money you each spend this week. At the end of the week look at your notes together and decide whether you're satisfied with how you are using your resources.

Chapter 64
Write Down the Numbers

Keep track of money regularly. Balance your checkbook(s), know your credit card balance(s), and be aware of large expenses and plan for them.

What you don't know about your own finances can hurt you. Lack of information leads to tension and unpleasant surprises. Knowing where you stand makes it easier to make beneficial decisions.

****

Your weekly assignment, should you choose to accept it:

Balance all your checkbooks. Make a list of all outstanding credit card balances and unpaid bills. Write down your total available cash and the total amount of money you owe. Either do this with your partner or share the information when you are each done.

Chapter 65
Use a System to Track Your Information

Use a computer system such as Quicken to track where your money is coming from and going to. You can use this information to make informed decisions about how to allocate or budget your resources.

When you make a commitment to pay attention to your finances, you almost automatically gain more control over your lives. When you discover how your money vanishes into unsuspected black holes, you will probably decide to make some changes.

****

Your weekly assignment, should you choose to accept it:

If you don't already have a system for keeping track of how you spend your money, create one now. Either purchase and install the software or use a paper system. If your system is already in place, review your spending for the past three months.

Chapter 66
Decide What Sharing Equitably Means

Decide on an equitable way to share resources and expenses. This can be especially tricky if you have very different income levels. Keep talking until you reach agreement.

There are many different ways to do this. One man asked his partner to turn over half her paycheck to him. In exchange, he gave her half of all he earned. Then they shared all expenses. Another couple chose to keep their money completely separate, and each paid certain joint expenses. They renegotiated frequently. Find a way that works for you.

****

Your weekly assignment, should you choose to accept it:

Each of you list three things that work and three things that don't work for you about the way you are sharing your resources and expenses now. Share your lists and decide if there's anything you would like to change.

Chapter 67

Negotiate and Renegotiate

Renegotiate financial agreements as your circumstances change. Changing paychecks, changing personal and family needs, and changing priorities all call for renegotiation.

Renegotiating means looking at how you're currently spending your money and whether this arrangement is helping you reach your goals. Then decide whether the new circumstances have led to new goals and whether a change in spending patterns is needed.

****

Your weekly assignment, should you choose to accept it:

Whether or not your circumstances have recently changed, evaluate whether the way you have spent your money in the past three months is helping you to reach your goals.

Chapter 68
Multiple Accounts Often Make Sense

Consider having both separate and joint accounts and decide which expenses will be paid from which account. Most people feel happier and more empowered when they don't need to account to anyone else about their personal spending.

There's no single formula that fits for every couple. Some couples contribute to a single account to cover joint expenses while keeping most of their income separate. Other couples divide the responsibility for paying different expenses.

****

Your weekly assignment, should you choose to accept it:

Discuss whether the system you are currently using is satisfactory for both of you. Even if it is, imagine using other options and see how you feel about them.

Chapter 69
Focus on Priorities

Create shared financial goals. Be sure you discuss and agree on priorities. If one of you thinks your savings are for a great vacation, and the other expects to use them to invest for financial independence, you are headed for trouble.

Talk about your dreams. Do you want to live in a big home or a small apartment? Travel or spend vacations at the same cottage each year? Send your children to Ivy League schools or the local junior college? Do you have entrepreneurial aspirations? Is simplicity your goal? Once you discuss and clarify your wishes, making decisions gets easier.

****

Your weekly assignment, should you choose to accept it:

Each of you list five things you want to be, do or have before you die, and five things you want to be, do or have in the next five years. Share your lists and interview each other about the reasons for your desires. "Just because" is a good enough answer, but the more information you can uncover about the dreams, the easier it will be to make them happen.

Chapter 70
Work with a Financial Advisor

Consult a financial advisor if your financial situation is complex, especially if one of you has substantially more resources than the other or if you are creating a blended family. Professional advice can help resolve money anxieties.

If you are avoiding this, it may be because it's uncomfortable to clarify your financial objectives and really examine your resources. You may feel embarrassed about sharing this sensitive information with your partner. It may be even more embarrassing to share it with a stranger. Nevertheless, it's very important.

****

Your weekly assignment, should you choose to accept it:

If you"ve already agreed to take this step and have not followed through, talk about why you are dragging your feet. When you're ready to take this step, ask people who are financially successful to recommend a trustworthy adviser.

Chapter 71
Getting Clear Is Better Than Getting Even

Forgot retaliation about money. If your partner spends money in a way that upsets you, discuss the problem, instead of going out and spending even more to get even with your partner.

Retaliation can lead to financial disaster. Upsets about how money is spent often mean that you do not have clear goals and guidelines about your financial life. Focus your conversation on establishing these goals and guidelines.

****

Your weekly assignment, should you choose to accept it:

Have a conversation about how your spending patterns either support or undermine your goals. Decide if any changes are necessary.

Chapter 72
Back to Basics — Spend Less, Save More

Spend less money than you make. Use the extra to build a reserve. Relieving money-related stress gives you energy for the things that really matter.

When you're constantly invited to spend money on things you don't need, just because you deserve them, it is easy lose track of your priorities. Pay attention to the long-term cost of short-term indulgences.

****

Your weekly assignment, should you choose to accept it:

List three things that you consider indulgences, one thing you do, one thing your partner does and one thing you do together. Share your lists, notice where you agree or disagree. Discuss the reasons those things are important to you and decide together whether to keep doing them.

Chapter 73
Share Responsibility

Share responsibility for financial decisions. Two heads are better than one, and when you are both responsible, neither of you is to blame if your results don't meet your expectations.

Even if you believe your partner knows much more than you do and even if you feel bored or overwhelmed at the very thought of managing your finances, do it anyway. If you are the knowledgeable and responsible side of the partnership, take time to help your partner understand your choices. It's worth the effort

****

Your weekly assignment, should you choose to accept it:

Together, review the part of your financial situation that you are reluctant to think about. It might be balancing your checkbook, or looking at how you spend your resources, or it might be reviewing your investments. Choose together, and just do it.

Chapter 74
Create Your Own Team

Accumulate a team of professional advisors. Find health, legal, financial and other resources before you need them.

Ask people you trust for referrals. You may wish to interview several different professionals in each field before you engage their services. This will also help you take your own financial situation more seriously.

****

Your weekly assignment, should you choose to accept it:

Have a conversation about the professionals that you each think you need. Make list of people you already know that you might want to interview. Then decide whom you will ask for references. Commit to make those inquiries and report your results to each other at a specific time.

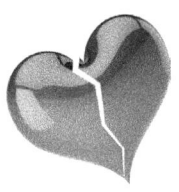

Part 9
Special Occasions

Automatically doing what you've done before causes problems. Thinking about what you each care about makes special occasions work better for both of you.

Chapter 75
Do It, even if It Seems Unimportant

Celebrate birthdays, anniversaries and holidays that are important to your partner, even if they are not important to you. Your partner's comfort will ultimately contribute to your own happiness.

Some people love to celebrate. To others, celebrations are completely irrelevant. It depends on your personal history and your personality style. Neither position is right; they're just different. It is usually more painful for a celebrator to miss a celebration then for a non-celebrator to participate in a celebration.

****

Your weekly assignment, should you choose to accept it:

Have a conversation about how your parents handled special occasions. Decide whether you are both happy with the way you are doing things. If you're not, talk about changes you could make.

Chapter 76
Ask for What YOU Want

Request that your partner celebrate special events in your life in the way that is most meaningful to you. Emphasize exactly what you want and how you want it, or your partner may not understand your needs.

If you want to be treated as if you are king or queen for a day on your birthday, and your partner does not think that birthdays are very important, you'll have to explain that you want breakfast in bed and a choice of activities designed to delight you. If you would rather open your presents on Christmas Eve than on Christmas morning you need to make that clear also.

You don't need to do something just because your partner wants you to, but when you get this kind of information, you do need to negotiate about what each of you is willing to do to please the other.

* * * * * * * * * * * * *

Your weekly assignment, should you choose to accept it:

Imagine what a perfect "special day" would be like for you. Tell your partner, in detail, exactly what you have imagined. Make agreements about what you will do for each other when those special days occur. Take notes and put them where you will find them to help you remember your agreements.

Chapter 77
Find a New Way

Create your own holiday traditions. You come from different families with different traditions. Choose what is most meaningful from each and combine them into something that will satisfy both of you.

If you loved the holiday traditions in your family of origin, you may need to continue them to feel comfortable and happy. However, if you were bored or impatient with them, now is the time to consider a change. If you are both passionate about mutually exclusive things, consider taking turns on alternate years.

****

Your weekly assignment, should you choose to accept it:

Each of you make a list of three things you loved, and three things you did not care about, or disliked in your family's celebration of the upcoming holiday. Share your lists and use them as the basis for deciding how you will celebrate this year.

Chapter 78
Meet the Family Visit Challenge

Clarify the obligations and priorities you each feel about visits with your extended families. Relationships with in-laws may be challenging for either of you.

To open the discussion, each of you can rate how comfortable you feel visiting your own family. Then rate how comfortable you feel visiting your partner's family. Use a scale of one to ten, with one being terrible and ten being wonderful. Use the same scale to respond to the statement: I get all the help and support I need from my partner when visiting my family. Next rate: I get all the help and support I need from my partner when visiting his/her family.

****

Your weekly assignment, should you choose to accept it:

Compare your responses to these statements, and if you discover any problem areas, discuss specific ways you would like help from each other in these situations. Then make realistic plans about what to do next time.

Chapter 79
Plan Ahead to Help Each Other

Offer special support to your partner during challenging family visits. Some people need more support in relating to their own parents and siblings than to their partner's families.

Probably neither one of you wants to discuss a situation in which one or both of you is going to be uncomfortable. However, if you talk about what makes you most uncomfortable, you can decide ahead of time how to take care of yourselves and each other.

****

Your weekly assignment, should you choose to accept it:

Talk about how you feel about spending time with each other's families. If there's been discomfort in the past, talk about what you could have done that would have made it easier for each of you. Use that to plan how you will manage your next visits.

Chapter 80

Celebrate Anything You Like

Develop your own special occasions. They can be to celebrate something you have experienced together or just because.

You can celebrate the anniversary of your first meeting, the first snowfall, your cat's birthday, paying off a charge card or cleaning out the garage. Celebrations are fun and help us wake up and notice the good things that happen to us.

****

Your weekly assignment, should you choose to accept it:

Pick something to celebrate together and do it today!

Chapter 81
Give a Hint, Take a Hint

Listen for hints about what gifts your partner would love to receive. Pay attention to what excites or delights your partner and use that information when you shop.

What you think your partner should want and what your partner actually wants can be extremely different. If your partner is blatant about it, s/he may take you to a store to visit the favorite, wished-for gift. If your partner is subtle, even asking his/her close friends may be helpful.

★★★★★★★★★★★★

Your weekly assignment, should you choose to accept it:

Talk together about creating wish lists. Go through catalogs together and mark all the things you each like. Make a clear agreement about whether you are just getting information or whether either of you actually expects to receive any of the objects you are looking at.

Chapter 82
Use Your Hints, Be a Hero

Give gifts that your partner has indicated that s/he wants or needs instead of what you believe s/he wants or needs. You can give other gifts too, but first paying attention to your partner avoids disappointment.

Some partners like to give each other hints about gifts they would like to receive. Others are very clear and forthright about asking for what they want. If you have not been paying attention to your partner's communication, now is a good time start.

****

Your weekly assignment, should you choose to accept it:

Have a conversation about how each of you lets the other know what is special and meaningful for you. Is your partner's method workable for you? If it isn't, talk about what would work, and decide what to do differently.

Chapter 83
Appreciate the Thought and Tell the Truth —Graciously

Create a mutually loving way to communicate when one of you receives a gift that doesn't work for you. Have this important conversation before, not after, a gift-giving occasion.

The truth is we all make mistakes. It can be very painful to find that a gift you have carefully selected for your partner is not being used or has been passed on to someone else. In the long run, it's easier to say gently, "I really appreciate your thoughtfulness, but I won't be able to use this because the style (color, size) doesn't really work for me. May I exchange it for something that does work?"

* * * * * * * * * * * * *

Your weekly assignment, should you choose to accept it:

Tell your partner what you do now when a gift doesn't work. Talk about how you would feel if your partner said the words I suggested to you. Decide what you will do in the future when a gift doesn't work.

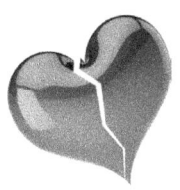

Part 10
Separateness

You don't have to either give up yourself to be in a relationship or give up the relationship in order to be yourself. Reclaim yourself to make your relationship stronger.

Chapter 84

Two Don't Become One

Keep your individuality while building your relationship. Two becoming one is an outmoded notion—it really means that each of you becomes half the person you were and is guaranteed to lead to resentment.

Giving up things that you love to do it order to spend more time together may seem tempting at first. You do need to accommodate to each other but hold on to the things that are especially meaningful to you.

****

Your weekly assignment, should you choose to accept it:

Think about things you used to do that you have not done in a long time. Share your lists with each other and notice whether there are things you each want to do individually when your partner does not want to do them with you.

Chapter 85
Be the Person You Are

Remember that you are a complete person and so is your partner. You are neither responsible for nor capable of completing each other.

It is nice to be able to focus on your strengths and delegate your weaknesses in a relationship. However, you will not be together all day every day for the rest of your lives. Remember that you, too, can cook, drive, call the plumber, plan a party or whatever you feel tempted to give up doing forever.

****

Your weekly assignment, should you choose to accept it:

Switch tasks or roles for a few hours. If your partner always plans social activities, you plan something for one evening. If you are used to asking your partner to fix broken things, make a serious attempt to fix something yourself. Ask your partner to teach you something that s/he is an expert at doing.

Chapter 86

It's OK to Do Some Things by Yourself

Encourage your partner to find ways do things s/he loves, even if you don't share the same interest. You do not have to do those things if they are uncomfortable for you. There is no rule that says you must do everything together.

When relationships are new, partners often try to please each other by giving up favorite activities. This sometimes leads to resentment or a nagging sense that something is missing. If you know that your partner has not seen an opera or gone skiing in a very long time because you don't enjoy that activity, suggest that s/he find a way to do it occasionally, without you.

****

Your weekly assignment, should you choose to accept it:

Talk to each other about activities you have each given up in order to please the other. Think of a way you can each experiment by doing something you used to enjoy and have not experienced in a long time.

Chapter 87
Help Each Other Grow and Change

Encourage your partner to grow and develop in his/her own way. This does not mean to chase your spouse around the house with a self-help book.

You may fear that if you grow, you will change into someone you don't recognize, and your partner doesn't love. You may fear that if your partner grows you will be left behind. This occasionally happens, but it's worth the risk. Growing and changing keeps your relationship alive.

****

Your weekly assignment, should you choose to accept it:

Each of you list three things you would like to learn in the next year. Share your lists and talk about how you can mutually support each other in learning at least one new thing. Then share your misgivings about the changes you will have to make to accomplish your new goals.

Chapter 88
Listen When You Want to Argue

Listen even when you disagree. Understanding your partner's position about something is not the same as agreeing with it.

Listening means letting your partner speak without interruption and focusing on what s/he is saying. Even if you have an internal emotional response, try not to let it show. Ask questions until you are sure you understand your partner's position.

****

Your weekly assignment, should you choose to accept it:

Take turns listening to each other describe a position you have argued about in the past. When you believe you understand your partner's position, tell your partner, "As I understand it, you believe that ..." When you have finished, ask your partner, "Is that actually your position?"

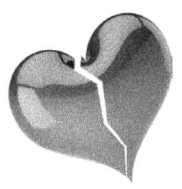

Part 11
Togetherness

Cherish the times you are together.
Use them to grow yourself and each other.

Chapter 89
It's Worth the Work

Spend time working on your relationship as well as living in the relationship. Good relationships don't just happen; they need to be watered and weeded, just like a garden.

Working on your relationship means taking some time on a regular basis to assess how the relationship is going. Sometimes spending five minutes every day works very well. Some partners take a few hours every quarter, and others take a week once a year. Some attend a couples retreat or workshop. Doing the homework assignments in this book also count as working on your relationship.

****

Your weekly assignment, should you choose to accept it:

Talk about what working on your relationship means to each of you. It may mean talking about your mutual and individual goals. It may mean looking at what irritates you or what you need in order to enhance your growth. Decide when and how you can best work on your relationship.

Chapter 90
Don't Wait, Live Now

Live your lives now. Don't wait until you get a better job, move to a new house, have a baby, or until the kids leave home—live now!

Suppose every day was a special day. What would you do differently? What are you putting off until tomorrow that you might be able to get started on today? Getting started on a dream makes it real to you, and that makes it more likely to happen.

****

Your weekly assignment, should you choose to accept it:

Make a list of things that you simply haven't gotten around to because you were too busy or because they seemed too big to tackle now. Share the list with your partner. Find small ways to get started on at least one special thing. That might mean checking travel Web sites or starting a special savings account that will allow you to make a down payment on the home of your dreams.

Chapter 91
Learn Something New Together

Attend classes and workshops together. Going through an adult education catalog and choosing what you would like to learn together is a good way to tune in to your partners interests.

Learning something new together will help you to keep the relationship alive and growing. Often, choosing something fun that neither of you know anything about, and that requires a minimum amount of time and/or money, is a good way to start.

****

Your weekly assignment, should you choose to accept it:

Get two copies of a local adult education catalog. (It could be a church bulletin.) Each of you independently mark classes that you are interested in attending. Compare your notes and see if there is any overlap.

Chapter 92
Ten Minutes Makes a Difference

Talk to each other for at least ten minutes a day about your daily successes, dreams, hopes, fears and disappointments. These important things sometimes get lost in the challenge of managing the logistics of complicated lives.

It is very easy to drift apart and take your partner for granted, assuming that nothing has changed because s/he has not mentioned that anything different is happening. When you take time to share your thoughts and feelings, you bridge the developing gap and move closer together.

****

Your weekly assignment, should you choose to accept it:

Take turns sharing at least one success each. Ask your partner questions about what that success means to him/her and what impact it will have in the future. Then repeat the process for dreams, hopes, fears and disappointments.

Chapter 93
Imagine Being Your Partner

Fill out magazine or on line questionnaires about your interests or personality pretending that you are your partner. Compare notes and see if you know your partner as well as you think you do.

Sometimes, you will find that you know each other very well. At other times, you may be very surprised at your partner's answers. In any case, you'll have a chance to think about each other and your relationship.

****

Your weekly assignment, should you choose to accept it:

Make four copies of any questionnaire. First, answer the questions for yourself, about yourself. Next, answer the questions the way you believe your partner would answer them. Now, each of you take a turn reading your partner's answer about you and your own answer about you for each question.

Chapter 94
Know Your Own Priorities and Your Partner's, too

Discuss your personal and joint priorities. Take time together periodically to make sure you're on track.

It's easy to lose track of your own goals and dreams in the bustle of everyday life. Urgent needs cry so loudly for attention that you can't hear the whispers of your own hearts. Take time to tune in.

****

Your weekly assignment, should you choose to accept it:

There are lots of great exercises to help you understand your own priorities. One is to set aside about thirty minutes and make a list of one hundred things you want to be sure you do in your lifetime. Write as fast as you can and repeat yourself as often as you wish. When you are done, review your list and share what you have learned with your partner.

Special Bonus: Long ago, my life partner and I recorded a powerful, forty-five-minute, life priority exercise while teaching a workshop. We have shared it with many people over the years. You can claim your own copy of the mp3 file at https://tinyurl.com/YourIdealDay.

You will need a stack of scratch paper and a writing implement.

Chapter 95
Practice Acts of Random Kindness

Do little things for each other, even if it's not a special occasion. Bring home flowers for no reason. Give your spouse a gift certificate for a round of golf, a facial, or a special favor from you, just because.

It is easy to fall into comfortable routines with each other. An unexpected gift or service, especially one that you know will delight your partner, says, I care! These small acts of kindness break the routine and bring you closer together.

****

Your weekly assignment, should you choose to accept it:

If you are uncertain about what would delight your partner, each of you list five to ten things you might do and ask the other if you are on the right track. If you are certain, choose something, and just do it!

Chapter 96
When Changes Rock the Boat—Rebalance

Expect major life changes to impact your relationship. Having a baby, losing a job, getting a new job, illness, death of a parent, retirement, etc., may create a need to renegotiate almost everything you thought was settled.

A major life change disrupts all your routines. You need different kinds of support from a partner, just at a time when your partner may be least available to you. This is the time to be extra sensitive to your partner, to be sure to ask your partner for what you need, and to be ready to negotiate.

****

Your weekly assignment, should you choose to accept it:

If you are anticipating a major life change, have a conversation about what you might need from each other when the change occurs. If you have recently experienced such a change, have a conversation about what you need from each other right now.

Chapter 97
Banish Blame

Avoid blaming your partner for a problem in your relationship. Address all problems as if you both contribute to them. You do!

The angrier you are about how your partner is acting, the more likely it is that you are doing something to contribute to the problem. Your contribution may have been avoiding talking about the problem in the past or overreacting. This can be difficult to sort out but is usually well worth the effort.

****

Your weekly assignment, should you choose to accept it:

Make a list of the things you do and do not do about a problem you have with your partner's behavior. Ask your partner what would happen if you changed your behavior by doing what you now don't do, or vice versa.

Chapter 98
Nurture Each Other

Feed each other. If only one of you has cooking skills, or only one of you has time to cook, reverse roles occasionally anyway. Feeding can be as simple as bringing your partner a cup of tea or offering to go out for ice cream.

Being fed is the original experience of being nurtured. For most people, it helps reduce tension and provides a sense of well-being. It's a simple but powerful action you can take to bring you closer together.

****

Your weekly assignment, should you choose to accept it:

Each of you list five different ways in which your partner can nurture you by feeding you. Review each other's lists and choose at least one thing to do immediately. Then make plans about what you will do to feed each other in the future.

Chapter 99

Heal Resentments

Play for favors. If either of you needs forgiveness for something you have done or failed to do, agree on a favor you can do that will heal the resentment.

It may be hard to forgive a mistake until something is done to fix both the problem that was caused by the mistake and the feelings you experienced because of needing to cope with the mistake. Candy, flowers, massages and toys can help make amends. If you need to be forgiven, ask your partner what will really help. Sometimes doing the laundry or getting the car serviced is what is really wanted.

* * * * * * * * * * * * *

Your weekly assignment, should you choose to accept it:

Think about what you would like your partner to do to heal any resentment you need to release. This means that when the favor is done, you will no longer feel resentful. Imagine different scenarios, and when you find one that will really work, talk it over with your partner. Your partner may offer alternate suggestions, but don't accept anything unless you will really experience it as healing. After you have agreed about what your partner will do to make amends, ask him/her to do it as soon as possible.

Chapter 100
Contribute Together

Support your partner in contributing to your community. Contributing time, money or energy to causes you both believe in will cement your relationship.

You probably are already a part of many different communities, such as workgroups, athletic groups, church groups and civic associations. When you contribute to these groups, you feel better about yourselves and have more to share with each other.

****

Your weekly assignment, should you choose to accept it:

If you feel that doing more for the community will be good for you, investigate opportunities to contribute to something together. If you are already over-committed, discuss ways to focus your energy only on the things that are most meaningful to you.

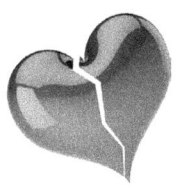

Part 12
Care of Your Partner

Keeping your partner well and happy is not your job. What you can do, though, is create conditions in which your partner can thrive.

Chapter 101
Affirm Positive Qualities

Remind your partner about the wonderful qualities s/he brings to your relationship. Remember what attracted you in the first place — personality, creativity, warmth, appearance, strength, feistiness, whatever.

It's easy to fall into the trap of just talking about problems. Positive affirmation is the lifeblood of a healthy relationship. Remember, the qualities that you pay attention to tend to increase.

****

Your weekly assignment, should you choose to accept it:

Make a list of at least five of your partner's positive qualities. Slip comments like, "You know, one of the reasons I love you is ..." into your conversations over the next few days.

Chapter 102
Affirm Appreciated Actions

Thank your partner for the routine things they do to make your life more pleasant. Does s/he wake you with a kiss and a cup of coffee or do the driving late at night when you are both tired? Remember to say thanks.

Noticing somebody doing something right instead of always focusing on what's wrong is contrary to what most of us experienced in school and in the workplace. Behavior that you pay attention to tends to be repeated, so if you want your partner to keep doing the things you enjoy, acknowledge them.

****

Your weekly assignment, should you choose to accept it:

Spend an entire week only talking to your partner about things you appreciate about him or her. Avoid talking about any problems. No-tice how you each feel at the end of the week.

Chapter 103
Deliver a Thoughtful Surprise

Surprise your partner with a special treat. It does not need to involve money. A massage, a library book by a favorite author, a walk to see some flowers that are just blooming or recording a special TV program can count as much as an expensive gift.

This is a great antidote to feeling taken for granted. It breaks the routine and lets your partner know that you care. It's especially useful when either of you has been involved in some intense activity.

****

Your weekly assignment, should you choose to accept it:

Do it today.

Chapter 104
Focus on What's Right

(This is another important variation of Tips 101 and 102).

Catch your partner doing something right and acknowledge it. It is easy to complain when something is wrong, but we tend to expect things to go right. Your recognition will be appreciated.

The reason that what you pay attention to increases is that most people love to be appreciated and will automatically repeat behavior in order to be appreciated again. This is a very useful strategy for times when you are especially irritated at your partner but don't want to talk about your anger.

* * * * * * * * * * * * *

Your weekly assignment, should you choose to accept it:

Make a list of at least 10 things your partner has done right in the past week. Put it aside and the next time you are angry about something you might criticize your partner for doing, review your list. Then decide what to do.

Chapter 105
Promise Only What You Will Deliver

Avoid disappointing your partner. Don't promise to do things just because your partner wants you to when you suspect you won't be able to keep the promise.

It often seems easier to say yes to something and hope your partner will forget about it, than to refuse a "reasonable" request. Sometimes, you even want to do it to please your partner, but you overestimate your ability to keep your agreement. You will both be happier if you only make promises you can and will keep.

****

Your weekly assignment, should you choose to accept it:

Each of you choose one thing you have promised to do, but that is still undone. Ask your partner what would happen if you never did it. If you decide to do it (based on your partner's response), make an agreement about when you will complete it, and keep your agreement. Otherwise, tell your partner that you will not do the task.

Chapter 106
Speak Your Positive Thoughts

Say aloud the nice things you think about your partner. Just because you think your partner already knows you care does not mean s/he would not like to hear about it.

It is easy to assume that your partner already knows how you feel, but often, this just isn't true. Both you and your partner probably hear more criticism than praise in the course of your week. Hearing nice things said aloud is a wonderful antidote for this.

****

Your weekly assignment, should you choose to accept it:

Pennies work here too. Put five pennies into one of your pockets. Every time you say something nice to your partner, shift a penny to a different pocket. Your goal is to shift all the pennies every day for an entire week.

Chapter 107
Connect with Hugs

Hug your partner frequently — not just when you want to get sexy. Touch is an important way that people use to know that they are loved.

A famous family therapist, Virginia Satir, said people need seven hugs a day just to maintain their health. How many are you getting now? How many would you like to get?

****

Your weekly assignment, should you choose to accept it:

Count the times you and your partner hug during the week. At the end of the week, decide whether you were sharing too few, too many, or just the right number of hugs. Plan any necessary changes.

Chapter 108
Speak in Your Partner's Love Language

Find out what makes your partner feel loved and do it frequently. Some people need time, others need touch, others need words of affirmation, others love gifts, and others feel loved when you do things for them.

Often you will try to show your love by giving your partner the very thing that makes you feel the most loved. When this works it's great. However, each partner usually has different needs, and neither of you understands why you don't seem to get what you need most.

****

Your weekly assignment, should you choose to accept it:

Have a conversation with your partner about what you each need to feel the most loved. Explain very specifically what your partner can do to please you.

Chapter 109
Discuss Important Concerns

Encourage your partner to get professional help if you think s/he needs it. Offer to go along, if that seems helpful.

It's easy to believe that a chronic problem is not that bad, because you have gotten used to it. You may be in a better position than your partner to know when help is needed. Tell your partner about your concerns and ask whether they are shared.

****

Your weekly assignment, should you choose to accept it:

Make an agreement that you will do this with each other when necessary. If there is a problem that either of you thinks needs attention, talk about it now.

Chapter 110
Just Listen and Be There

Support your partner by listening to him/her express feelings of sadness about a loss. You probably can't fix the loss or solve the problem, but just being close will help the healing process.

You may feel uncomfortable just listening to a problem without trying to help your partner to fix it. You may even want to tell your partner to get over it instead of moping around and feeling bad. Neither of these approaches is nearly as helpful as just listening attentively.

****

Your weekly assignment, should you choose to accept it:

Talk about how you have helped each other manage losses in the past. Discuss how each of you felt in those situations and whether you need to try something new next time.

Chapter 111
Be Truthful About Time

Estimate your time commitments accurately. Tell your partner what time you are most likely to be home instead of when you hope you will be home (if traffic is not too busy and you make all the lights).

It's a very easy to tell your partner what you think he/she would like to hear. Giving misinformation may avoid temporary disappointment, but it will create mistrust in the long run. Tell the truth even if you know your partner won't like it.

****

Your weekly assignment, should you choose to accept it:

Practice being scrupulously honest about your time agreements with your partner for an entire week. Notice whether this is different than your ordinary behavior. Decide together whether you will make any changes in how you communicate about time after the week is over.

Chapter 112
Compliment Publicly, Complain Privately

Compliment your partner in public; complain only in private.

This time-tested management principle is important in every kind of relationship. Whatever others hear is magnified. Public praise makes you glow. Public criticism can magnify the receiver's hurt more than you can imagine.

****

Your weekly assignment, should you choose to accept it:

Give your partner a public compliment. Tell him/her about something you appreciate where others can hear you or tell someone else something great about your partner when your partner is present.

Chapter 113
Get Consultation When You Need It

If you have a problem with your partner, talk about it together. If you need advice about how to discuss a problem, ask a trusted advisor privately.

Sometimes it's hard to figure out how to approach your partner about a sensitive issue. Instead of just keeping silent or complaining to someone else about the situation, talk it through with someone who will help you figure out what to do. Choose someone who will respect your privacy and keep your talk confidential.

****

Your weekly assignment, should you choose to accept it:

Either discuss an unsolved problem with your partner or decide who can help you figure out how to have that discussion. Make plans about how to get any help you may need.

Chapter 114
Apologize, even if It Was an Accident

Say, "I'm sorry," when you accidentally hurt your partner instead of explaining why s/he should not be hurt because you didn't mean to cause any harm. Sometimes, that's all it takes to fix the problem.

Often, we step on each other's toes without meaning to. However, the injured toes still hurt. An apology for the hurt instead of a defensive reaction is helpful. Offering to do something nice to make up for accidentally causing a problem will often help even more.

****

Your weekly assignment, should you choose to accept it:

If either of you is feeling resentful about something your partner has done, even if it was just the result of an accidental or thoughtless action, think about what apology or restitution you would like. Share this with your partner and decide how to solve the problem.

Chapter 115

Listen Intensely

Give your partner the greatest gift you can give another person. Listen to him/her with your full attention.

Often, what passes for listening is planning what you intend to say in response to what your partner tells you. Sometimes, it means impatiently waiting for your own turn or listening while doing something else that is occupying your partial attention. Just listening really is worth the effort.

****

Your weekly assignment, should you choose to accept it:

Learning to just listen may take some practice. Set aside a few minutes for one of you to tell the other your thoughts or feelings — about anything. Show that you are listening by watching your partner while s/he is speaking. When your partner is done, ask, "Is there anything else?" When your partner is really finished, you can simply summarize what you have heard. Trade speaker and listener roles at another time.

Chapter 116
Accept Your Partner's Feelings

Honor your partner's report of how s/he feels. Insisting that s/he does or should feel differently about anything is like saying you understand your partner better than s/he understands him/herself. You don't!

The truth is probably that YOU wish that your partner felt differently. Feelings are temporary responses to life imbalances. Asking questions about the reasons your partner feels as s/he does will help both of you understand the situation.

****

Your weekly assignment, should you choose to accept it:

Have a conversation with your partner about whether this is a problem for either of you. If it is, practice looking at the reasons for feelings together. Make an agreement to alert each other any time the problem recurs.

Chapter 117
Empower Aliveness

Empower your partner to seek his/her own happiness. It's not your responsibility, nor is it within your power, to make your partner happy.

Empowering sometimes means encouraging each other to notice the activities and experiences that make each of you feel most alive. Sometimes, it means allowing each other space and time to explore new directions without interference.

★★★★★★★★★★★★★

Your weekly assignment, should you choose to accept it:

Each of you write the statement: What really makes me happy is_____. Then continue writing as many ways to complete the statement as you can think of for ten minutes. Write quickly without thinking or editing. Talk to each other about what you have written.

Chapter 118
Avoid Known Sore Spots

Avoid doing anything that you know from experience will cause your partner pain. If you feel you must do it anyway for some reason, discuss it ahead of time with your partner and see if, working together, you can find a way to minimize the pain.

Something that is completely innocuous for one person may unknowingly remind the other of a painful, long ago, experience. When you bring it up, it may feel like rubbing salt in a wound. The first time this happens is usually accidental. Notice those accidents and avoid repeating them.

****

Your weekly assignment, should you choose to accept it:

If you need to discuss a painful subject, tell your partner why you feel a need to have the discussion. Next, ask your partner if and when s/he is willing to have the discussion. If your partner says no, respect his/her wishes and try again at another time.

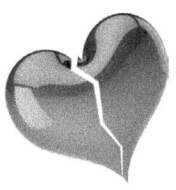

Part 13

Self-Care

Taking good care of yourself is your own responsibility. It is always OK to ask for help and support when doing this crucial job.

Chapter 119
Remember Your Favorite Things

Do whatever makes you feel vibrant and alive, even if you need to do it alone. When you feel vibrant and alive, you are attractive to your partner and to others.

Doing necessary activities often make you lose track of doing those important activities that contribute to your emotional and spiritual well-being. Making time for special things may seem selfish. It's not. The long-term benefits are worth it.

****

Your weekly assignment, should you choose to accept it:

Each of you make a list of twenty-five things you love to do. Then note how long it has been since you've done each of them. Discuss your lists with each other and create a list of things you would like to do together. Choose something from the remaining items on your own list and create a plan about when you can do that, too.

Chapter 120
Include Your Personal Goals

Take responsibility for arranging to get what you need and want in your life. This is not your partner's job, although s/he may be happy to help you in your quest if you communicate it clearly and request help.

Whether you want to go back to school, learn to play tennis, see a concert, change careers, get a pedicure or have the laundry done, do something to move yourself toward that goal. It can be as simple as making a phone call or checking information on the Internet. Tell your partner what you are doing.

★ ★ ★ ★ ★ ★ ★ ★ ★ ★ ★ ★ ★

Your weekly assignment, should you choose to accept it:

Make a wish list containing at least three items. Share your list with your partner and imagine together how doing what you wish for would impact your lives.

Chapter 121
Ask for Recognition

Make sure you ask for the acknowledgment you want from your partner. If your partner does not notice your new haircut or the amount of work you did to arrange an event, say something instead of waiting for your compliments.

Spontaneous recognition is wonderful. Some people do it well, but it simply may not occur to your partner that you need or want any acknowledgement at all. Your partner may be quite happy to give you the attention you want, once s/he understands that you want it. The recognition you get only after you ask for it still feels good.

****

Your weekly assignment, should you choose to accept it:

Each of you choose three things you wish the other had acknowledged you for. Take turns choosing one item from your list and telling you partner about it. Then say, "I wanted you to notice it and ...hug me...cheer for me...tell me you are proud of me...bring me flowers...etc. Will you do that for me NOW?"

Chapter 122
Let a Professional Help

Get help when you need it. If you feel stuck, depressed or upset for more than a couple of weeks, talk to someone (a counselor, coach or other trained professional) who can help.

Sometimes things that are mysterious to you are obvious to a trained professional who could quickly help you sort out the problem. If you don't know whom to talk to, ask a good friend, a health-care professional or clergyperson to recommend someone.

* * * * * * * * * * * * *

Your weekly assignment, should you choose to accept it:

Each of you answer this question for your partner. In the last year, have you felt anxious, depressed or upset for more than a week or two at a time? If necessary, talk about the details and decide what to do next.

Chapter 123
Think Before You Say Yes (or No)

Consider whether or not you will do something your partner wants and you don't. Sometimes, doing something you do not especially want to do for your partner costs you very little in time or inconvenience and is very important to your partner. Sometimes, it is very expensive emotionally.

If you decide not to do something your partner wants you to do, explain the reasons for your choice. If you choose to comply with your partner's request, tell your partner the truth, "I don't especially want to do this, but I am willing to do it because it's important to you."

****

Your weekly assignment, should you choose to accept it:

When your partner asks you to do something that you ordinarily don't do, take a few extra minutes to think about whether it's something that you really want to do. Tell your partner, "I need to think about this for a moment." Then tell your partner what you've decided and why.

Chapter 124
Pay Attention to Your Intuition

Trust your hunches enough to check them out. If you suspect that something is wrong, for either of you, talk about it. Everyone makes up stories about small bits of barely noticed information—stories which may or may not be true.

If you let your hunch turn into a belief or conviction before you check it out, you may believe you have information when you really don't. You may then do or say things you will later regret. On the other hand, your hunch might turn out to be an accurate early warning of a developing problem. Talk!

****

Your weekly assignment, should you choose to accept it:

Talk to each other about hunches you have had in the past. Notice if they turned out to be important warnings or just old fears stimulated by misunderstood experiences. If you have any current hunches, discuss these also.

Chapter 125
Remember to Make Yourself a Priority

Make taking good care of yourself a priority. In airplanes, you are reminded to put on your own oxygen mask first, before you assist others. In relationships, taking care of yourself regularly enables you to fully engage with your partner.

Taking care of yourself means doing things that build up your own energy. They might include exercising regularly, seeing your friends or making sure that you do activities you love even if your partner is not interested in them.

****

Your weekly assignment, should you choose to accept it:

List ten things that you can do that build your own energy and make you feel good about yourself. Make plans to do one or two of them in the next week.

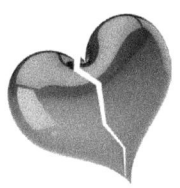

Part 14
Your Relationship Is Worth It!

Cultural myths and misinformation prevent people from having the loving relationships they deserve.

- Great relationships are not made in heaven.
- They do not need to end when you fall out of love.
- Great relationships are not always exciting.
- They are not limited to a few lucky people.

Great relationships do require:

- Information
- Attention
- Time (less than an hour a week)
- Commitment to the challenge of creating them

Use these tools to help have the conversations that build your own great relationship.

**

You'll find links to all the *Secrets of Happy Relationship Series* books at www.BooksByLaurie.com. Go there now and order the next book you need to create the happy relationship you want and deserve.

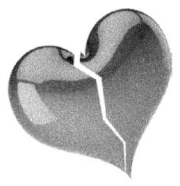

Special Bonus Reminder

If you have not yet claimed your bonus gift, do it now.

Listen to a wide-ranging conversation about relationships as radio host Steve Toth interviews Dr. Laurie Weiss on his *Mind, Body and Spirit* radio show.

Discover:

- Mistaken beliefs that destroy relationships
- How caring confrontation creates better communication
- Hidden agendas that lead to arguments
- Why really listening is important
- How clarifying values helps end arguments

Download your 47-minute MP3 file here and listen today.

www.BooksByLaurie.com/SteveToth

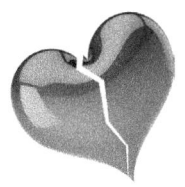

Please Help Me Reach New Readers

Chances are that you checked out the reviews on this book when you purchased it. Reviews are critical to help prospective readers decide to read books. I would be thrilled if you would leave a review NOW, while you are thinking about it.

If you are someone who has done this before, you know how easy it is.

If you're not, you may be shuddering at the memory of grade school book reviews. This is different!!! Really it is!

All you need to do is imagine that you are telling a friend about reading this book. Then follow these steps.

- Say what you would tell your friend into your phone and record it in the notes section and let your phone write it out. (All you need to say is one or two sentences.)

- Email it to yourself.

- Add punctuation if necessary.

Cut and paste your sentences into a review box wherever you buy your books.

I have included a few links to popular places to leave your reviews. Go to www.BooksByLaurie.com or www.Goodreads.com/Laurie_Weiss and click on any book title. Scroll down to find the instructions to leave a review.

I would love to hear from you about how this book impacted you. And, if you have any problems or questions about this book I would really appreciate hearing from you directly. My email address is Laurie@LaurieWeiss.com . You will find my phone number and social media connections on another page.

BEING HAPPY TOGETHER

Thank you in advance for taking the time to contribute to the conversation about what to read. I truly appreciate it.

Laurie

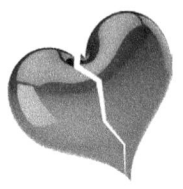

About the Author

Women have been asking Dr. Laurie Weiss questions about relationships for over 45 years. Now she shares her answers to some of them with you.

Relationship Communication Expert, Dr. Laurie Weiss, is internationally known as an expert who helps other relationship consultation professionals develop their skills.

As a psychotherapist, coach, marriage counselor, author and stress-relief expert she has helped more than 60,000 individuals reclaim life energy and find joy in life for more than four decades. She has taught professionals in 13 countries and authored eight books that make complex information accessible to anyone. Her latest, ***Letting It Go***, teaches rapid anxiety and stress relief. http://www.Laurie Weiss.com

Dr. Weiss is one of only two Master Certified Logosynthesis Practitioners in the United States. She is a Certified Transactional Analysis Trainer with Clinical and Organizational Specialties and a Master Certified Coach. Her work has been translated into German, Chinese, Spanish, French and Portuguese.

She is passionate about helping people have the important conversations that build great personal and working relationships. She says, "I have an unshakeable belief, based on over 45 years of experience, that people are doing the very best they can with the resources they have available to them at any given moment."

Dr. Laurie and her husband, Dr. Jonathan B. Weiss, started working together in 1970. Both Drs. Weiss love mixing business and pleasure and enjoy visiting professional colleagues and friends around the globe. They live and work in Littleton, CO, USA.

She loves adventures, went indoor skydiving for the first time at age 67 and zip lining for the first time at age 75. She has been blessed by elephants in India, walked on hot coals, visited Camelot, flown over the Pyramids, and spent an afternoon at the sex temples at Khajiraho and learned more possible sex positions than she can possibly remember.

E-mail: Laurie@LaurieWeiss.com

Office: 303-794-5379

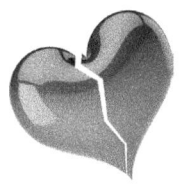

How to Work With Dr. Laurie

My husband, Dr. Jonathan B. Weiss and I have been married since 1960 and business partners since 1972 when we were teaching Transactional Analysis throughout the United States. We have been learning and teaching cutting edge tools for healing and transformation for over 45 years.

We have both been Teaching and Supervising Transactional Analysts for over four decades. Currently we are the only Certified Logosynthesis Practitioners in the United States. Either or both of us would be delighted to help you learn more about creating joy and satisfaction in your life and your important relationships.

Contact Us: We Usually Answer the Phone

DR. LAURIE WEISS

You can contact us directly to discuss what is best for you and your group. We offer a variety of options including CLASSES, TALKS, BOOK GROUP VISITS, PROFESSIONAL CONFERENCE PRESENTATIONS, TRAINING, INDIVIDUAL and COUPLES APPOINTMENTS. We work with our clients in person, by phone and by Skype.

Dr. Laurie Weiss:

LaurieWeiss@EmpowermentSystems.com

Dr. Jonathan Weiss: Weiss@EmpowermentSystems.com

Empowerment Systems

506 West Davies Way

Littleton, CO 80120 USA

303-794-5379

Websites

Personal: http://www.LaurieWeiss.com

Logosynthesis: http://www.LogosynthesisColorado.com

Business: http://www.EmpowermentSystems.com

Purchase Books: http://www.BooksbyLaurie.com

Social Media

Facebook: https://www.Facebook.com/laurieweiss

LinkedIn: http://www.Linkedin.com/in/laurieweiss

Pinterest: https://www.Pinterest.com/laurieweiss/

Twitter: https://Twitter.com/@LaurieWeiss

Goodreads: https://www.Goodreads.com/Laurie_Weiss

DR. LAURIE WEISS

Blogs

Personal Development:
http://www.IDontNeedTherapy.com/blog

Relationship: http://RelationshipHQ.com/blog/

Business Communication:
http://www.DareToSayIt.com/blog

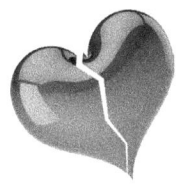

About the Secrets of Happy Relationships Series

Relationships aren't easy. Relationships are often confused and messy with partners trying to find happiness in all the wrong ways.

Real relationships get messy because even though you think your life partner is just like you, he or she isn't. You are two different people trying to meet the challenge of creating and maintaining a happy and loving relationship, perhaps without much useful information.

To make matters worse, you live in the midst of the outmoded role expectations of a culture that values drama and competition and extreme busyness. Most media doesn't help. It focuses on difficult relationships, not successful ones.

Dr. Laurie Weiss

Ordinary relationships have their ups and downs and almost nobody writes about those cycles. It's no wonder there are so many misunderstandings. Creating a lasting, loving, growing relationship is an incredible challenge. It's completely natural to have questions about your relationship.

I've been answering questions about relationships since 1973 when I was in newly minted TA (Transactional Analysis) therapist and was sure I had the answers to all the problems of the world. I had been married for 13 years and we had survived some major challenges. I was happily learning and using our new tools. Over four decades later, we are still married, and I've learned a lot.

It's been my pleasure and privilege to help people sort out the misconceptions, misunderstandings and challenges of creating happy, loving relationships. Being happy together is a gift my husband and I have given each other through the work of addressing issues as they arise. It's a gift you can have also; by giving it to each other.

Books in the Secrets of Happy Relationships Series

Are You My Perfect Partner?
To Marry or Not to Marry …
Are you really ready to get married?

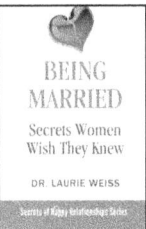

Being Married:
Secrets Women Wish They Knew
*Crucial information you need
to know about marriage*

Stop Poisoning Your Marriage
with These Common Beliefs
*Are you letting these myths
undermine your marriage?*

Dr. Laurie Weiss

Relationship Tips for Life Partners
Critical guidelines for creating a true partnership

Reconnect to Rescue Your Marriage:
Avoid Divorce and Feel Loved Again
What to do before leaving your troubled marriage

Stop Arguing and Start Talking …
even if you are afraid your only answer is divorce!
Are you ready to have these loving,
productive conversations with your spouse?

Being Happy Together:
What to Do to Keep Love Alive
Unlock secrets to rapid relationship
renewal in just an hour a week

Other Books by Laurie Weiss

Letting It Go: Relieve Anxiety and Toxic
Stress in Just a Few Minutes Using Only Words
(Rapid Relief with Logosynthesis®)
*Are you ready for relaxation to replace
anxiety in your life?*

Emotional Self-Help: I Don't Need Therapy,
But Where Do I Turn for Answers?
Do you need to become emotionally literate?
www.BooksByLaurie.com/answers

Recovery From CoDependency:
It's Never Too Late To Reclaim Your Childhood
Are you ready to release your codependency?
www.BooksByLaurie.com/recovery

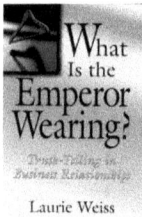

**An Action Plan for Your Inner Child:
Parenting Each Other**
Are you ready to reclaim your inner child?
https://www.amazon.com/dp/1558741658

**What Is the Emperor Wearing?
Truth-Telling in Business Relationships**
Do you wish you dared to tell the truth?
www.BooksByLaurie.com/emperor

www.ingramcontent.com/pod-product-compliance
Lightning Source LLC
Chambersburg PA
CBHW051546020426
42333CB00016B/2119